Verbs

Verbs

VERBS

T.C. Abraham

Commonwealth

Verbs

First Published : 2009

ISBN 978-81-311-0219-0

Published by :
COMMONWEALTH PUBLISHERS PVT. LTD.
4831/24, Prahlad Street,
Ansari Road, Darya Ganj,
New Delhi - 110002
Ph. : 23272541, 23257835
Fax : 91- 011- 23257835
e-mail : campusbooks@hotmail.com

Laser Typesetting by :
Dimple Typesetter
Delhi

Printed at :
Roshan Offset Printers
Delhi

Preface

A verb is defined as a word which describes what a subject does or what was done to the subject. The world verb is from the Latin *verbum,* meaning "word"—short, one way suppose, for "action word". Verbs have many sub-categories in all languages and just as nouns are the heads of verb phrases that may include as additional material such as articles and modifiers of various sorts, verbs are the heads of verb phrases that may include noun phrases as objects and other kinds of additional material that fill out the meaning of the verb. An essential part of speech, a knowledge verbs in an essential part of grammar learning that makes possible for one to comprehend the intricacies of a language.

The present text has been written as a manual on the verbs of English grammar. The text, however, is not a mere compendium of the types of verbs, or the rules which define their use; rather, it concentrates on providing readers with a manual on the ways in which verbs are practiced. Incorporating a comprehensive content, it supplements this information by providing numerous practices exercises which should provide readers with the opportunity to hone their skills in verb use.

T.C. Abraham

Contents

Contents

1

Introduction

Verbs in the English language are a lexically and morphologically distinct part of speech which describes an action, an event, or a state. While English has many irregular verbs, for the regular ones the conjugation rules are quite straightforward.

The verb is perhaps the most important part of the sentence. A verb or compound verb asserts something about the subject of the sentence and express actions, events, or states of being. The verb or compound verb is the critical element of the predicate of a sentence.

In each of the following sentences, the verb or compound verb is highlighted:

Dracula *bites* his victims on the neck.

The verb "bites" describes the action Dracula takes.

In early October, Giselle *will plant* twenty tulip bulbs.

Here the compound verb "will plant" describes an action that will take place in the future.

My first teacher *was* Miss Crawford, but I remember the janitor Mr. Weatherbee more vividly.

In this sentence, the verb "was" (the simple past tense of "is") identifies a particular person and the verb "remembered" describes a mental action.

Karl Creelman bicycled around the world in 1899, but his diaries and his bicycle *were destroyed.*

In this sentence, the compound verb "were destroyed" describes an action which took place in the past.

PARTS OF VERB

A regular English verb has only one principal part, the infinitive or dictionary form (which is identical to the simple present tense for all persons and numbers except the third person singular). All other forms of a regular verb can be derived straight-forwardly from the infinitive, for a total of four forms (e.g. exist, exists, existed, existing)

English irregular verbs have at most three principal parts:

Part	*Example*
1. infinitive	write
2. preterite	wrote
3. past participle	written

Strong verbs like write have all three distinct parts, for a total of five forms. The more irregular weak verbs also require up to three forms to be learned.

The highly irregular copular verb to be has eight forms: be, am, is, are, being, was, were, been, of which only one is derivable from a principal part (being is derived from be).

Verbs had more forms when the pronoun thou was still in regular use and there was a number distinction in the second person. To be, for instance, had art, wast and wert.

Most of the strong verbs that survive in modern English are considered irregular. Irregular verbs in English come from several historical sources; some are technically strong verbs; others have had various phonetic changes or contractions added to them over the history of English.

INFINITIVE AND BASIC FORM

Formation

The infinitive in English is the naked root form of the word. When it is being used as a verbal noun, the particle to is usually prefixed to it. When the infinitive stands as the predicate of an auxiliary verb, to may be omitted, depending on the requirements of the idiom.

Uses

— The infinitive, in English, is one of two verbal nouns: To write is to learn.

— The infinitive, either marked with to or unmarked, is used as the complement of many auxiliary verbs: *I will write a novel about talking beavers; I am really going to write it.*

— The basic form also forms the English imperative mood: Write these words.

— The basic form makes the English subjunctive mood: *If you write it, they will read.*

THIRD PERSON SINGULAR

Formation

The third person singular in regular verbs in English is distinguished by the suffix -s. In English spelling, this -s is added to the stem of the infinitive form: run → runs.

If the base ends in a sibilant sound like /s/, /z/ that is not followed by a silent E, the suffix is written -es: buzz→buzzes; catch→catches.

If the base ends in a consonant plus y, the y changes to an i and -es is affixed to the end: cry →cries.

Verbs ending in o typically add es: veto →vetoes.

The third person singular present indicative in English is notable cross-linguistically for being a morphologically marked form for a semantically unmarked one. That is to say the third person singular is usually taken to be the most basic form in a given verbal category and as such, according to markedness theory, should have the simplest of forms in its paradigm. This is clearly not the case with English where the other persons exhibit the bare root and nothing more. In Early Modern English, some dialects distinguished the third person singular with the suffix -th; after consonants this was written -eth, and some consonants were doubled when this was added: run → runneth.

Usage

The third person singular is used exclusively in the third person form of the English simple "present tense", which often has other uses besides the simple present: *He writes airport novels about anthropomorphic rodents.*

Exception

English preserves a number of preterite-present verbs, such as can and may. These verbs lack a separate form for the third person singular: she can, she may. All surviving preterite-present verbs in modern English are auxiliary verbs. The verb will, although historically not a preterite-present verb, has come to be inflected like one when used as an auxiliary; it adds -s in the third person singular only when it is a full verb: *Whatever she wills to happen will make life annoying for everyone else.*

PRESENT PARTICIPLE

Formation

The present participle is made by the suffix -ing: go →going.

If the base ends in silent e, it is dropped before adding the suffix: believe → believing.

If the e is not silent, it is retained: agree → agreeing.

If the base ends in -ie, change the ie to y and add -ing: lie → lying.

If:

— the base form ends in a single consonant; and

— a single vowel precedes that consonant; and

— the last syllable of the base form is stressed

Then the final consonant is doubled before adding the suffix: set → setting; occur → occurring.

In British English, as an exception, the final <l> is subject to doubling even when the last syllable is not stressed: yodel → yodelling, travel → travelling; in American English, these follow the rule: yodeling, traveling.

Irregular forms include:

- singeing, where the e is (sometimes) not dropped to avoid confusion with singing;
- ageing, in British English, where the expected form aging is ambiguous as to whether it has a hard or soft g;
- words ending in -c, which add k before the -ing, for example, trafficking, panicking, frolicking, and bivouacking.
- a number of words that are subject to the doubling rule even though they do not fall squarely within its terms, such as diagramming, kidnapping, programming, and worshipping.

Uses

The present participle is another English verbal noun: Writing is learning.

It is used as an adjective: a writing desk; building beavers.

It is used to form a past, present or future tense with progressive or imperfective force: *He is writing another long book about beavers.* It is used with quasi-auxiliaries to form verb phrases: *He tried writing about opossums instead, but his muse deserted him.*

PRETERITE

Formation

In weak verbs, the preterite is formed with the suffix -ed: work → worked.

If the base ends in e, -d is simply added to it: hone → honed; dye → dyed.

Where the base ends in a consonant plus y, the y changes to i before the -ed is added; deny → denied.

Where the base ends in a vowel plus y, the y is retained: alloy → alloyed.

The rule for doubling the final consonant in regular weak verbs for the preterite is the same as the rule for doubling in the present participle,

Use

The preterite is used for the English simple past tense. *He wrote two more chapters about the dam at Kashagawigamog Lake.*

PAST PARTICIPLE

Formation

In regular weak verbs, the past participle is always the same as the preterite. Irregular verbs may have separate preterites and past participles.

Uses

The past participle is used with the auxiliary have for the English perfect tenses: They have written about the slap of tails on water, about the scent of the lodge. With verbs of motion, an archaic form with be may be found in older texts: he is come. With be, it forms the passive voice: It is written so well, you can feel what it is like to gnaw down trees! It is used as an adjective: *the written word; a broken dam.* It is used with quasi-auxiliaries to form verb phrases: *five hundred thousand words got written in record time.*

GROUPS OF VERBS

Before you begin the verb tense lessons, it is extremely important to understand that not all English verbs are the same. English verbs are divided into three groups: Normal Verbs, Non-Continuous Verbs, and Mixed Verbs.

Group I Normal Verbs

Most verbs are "Normal Verbs." These verbs are usually physical actions which you can see somebody doing. These verbs can be used in all tenses.

Normal Verbs

to run, to walk, to eat, to fly, to go, to say, to touch, etc.

Examples:

— *I eat dinner every day.*

— *I am eating dinner now.*

Group II Non-Continuous Verbs

The second group, called "Non-Continuous Verbs," is smaller. These verbs are usually things you cannot see somebody doing. These verbs are rarely used in continuous tenses. They include:

Abstract Verbs

to be, to want, to cost, to seem, to need, to care, to contain, to owe, to exist...

Possession Verbs

to possess, to own, to belong...

Emotion Verbs

to like, to love, to hate, to dislike, to fear, to envy, to mind...

Examples:

— *He is needing help now.* Not Correct

— *He needs help now.* Correct

— *He is wanting a drink now.* Not Correct

— *He wants a drink now.* Correct

Group III Mixed Verbs

The third group, called "Mixed Verbs," is the smallest group. These verbs have more than one meaning. In a way, each meaning is a unique verb. Some meanings behave like "Non-Continuous Verbs," while other meanings behave like "Normal Verbs."

Mixed Verbs

to appear, to feel, to have, to hear, to look, to see, to weigh..

Mixed nerbs with examples and definitions:

To appear:

— Donna appears confused. *Non-Continuous Verb*

Donna seems confused.

— My favorite singer is appearing at the jazz club tonight. *Normal verb*

My favorite singer is giving a performance at the jazz club tonight.

To have:

— I have a dollar now. *Non-continuous verb*

I possess a dollar.

— I am having fun now. *Normal verb*

I am experiencing fun now.

To hear:

— She hears the music. *Non-continuous verb*

She hears the music with her ears.

— She is hearing voices. *Normal verb*

She hears something others cannot hear. She is hearing voices in her mind.

To look:

— nancy looks tired. *Non-continuous verb*

She seems tired.

— Farah is looking at the pictures. *Normal verb*

She is looking with her eyes.

To miss:

— john misses sally. *Non-continuous verb*

He is sad because she is not there.

— debbie is missing her favorite tv program. Normal verb

She is not there to see her favorite program.

To see:

— I see her. *Non-continuous verb*

I see her with my eyes.

— I am seeing the doctor. *Normal verb*

I am visiting or consulting with a doctor.

— I am seeing her. *Normal verb*

I am having a relationship with her.

— He is seeing ghosts at night. *Normal verb*

He sees something others cannot see. For example ghosts, aura, a vision of the future, etc.

To smell:

— The coffee smells good. *Non-continuous verb*

The coffee has a good smell.

— I am smelling the flowers. *Normal verb*

I am sniffing the flowers to see what their smell is like.

To taste:

— the coffee tastes good. *Non-continuous verb*

The coffee has a good taste.

— I am tasting the cake. Normal verb

I am trying the cake to see what it tastes like.

To think:

— He thinks the test is easy. Non-continuous verb

He considers the test to be easy.

— She is thinking about the question. Normal verb

She is pondering the question, going over it in her mind.

To weigh:

— The table weighs a lot. Non-continuous verb

The table is heavy.

— She is weighing herself. Normal verb

She is determining her weight.

Some verbs can be especially confusing:

To be:

— Joe is american. Non-continuous verb

Joe is an american citizen.

— Joe is being very american. Normal verb

Joe is behaving like a stereotypical american.

— joe is being very rude. Normal verb

Joe is behaving very rudely. Usually he is not rude.

— Joe is being very formal. Normal verb

Joe is behaving very formally. Usually he is not formal.

Notice: Only rarely is "to be" used in a continuous form. This is most commonly done when a person is temporarily behaving badly or stereotypically. It can also be used when someone's behavior is noticeably different.

2

Regular and Irregular Verbs

REGULAR VERBS

A regular verb is any verb whose conjugation follows the typical grammatical inflections of the language it belongs to. A verb that cannot be conjugated like this is called an irregular verb. All natural languages, to different extents, have a number of irregular verbs. Auxiliary languages usually have a single regular pattern for all verbs (as well as other parts of speech) as a matter of design. Other constructed languages need not show such regularity, especially if they are designed to look similar to natural ones.

The most simple form of regularity involves a single class of verbs, a single principal part (the root or a conjugated form in a given person, number, tense, aspect, mood, etc.), and a set of unique rules to produce each form in the verb paradigm. More complex regular patterns may have several verb classes (e. g. distinguished by their infinitive ending), more than one principal part (e. g. the infinitive and the first person singular, present tense, indicative mood), and more than one type of rule (e. g. rules that add suffixes and other rules that change the vowel in the root).

Sometimes it is highly subjective to state whether a verb is regular or not. For example, if a language has ten different conjugation patterns and two of them only comprise five or six verbs each while the rest are much more populated, it is a matter of choice to call the verbs in the smaller groups "irregular".

The concept of regular and irregular verbs belongs mainly in the context of second language acquisition, where the defining of rules and listing of exceptions is an important part of foreign language learning. The concepts can also be useful in psycholinguistics, where the ways in which the human mind processes irregularities may be of interest. However, most other branches of linguistics do not use these categories; historical/comparative linguistics is more interested in categories such as strong and weak.

Regular verbs are formed by an –ed suffix on the verb.

work	worked	worked	(pronounced/t/)
live	lived	lived	(pronounced /d /)
wait	waited	waited	(pronounced /Id/)

The pronunciation /t/ occurs when the verb ends in the sounds /f/, /k/, /p/, /s/, /S/,/tS/ as in reach, /T / as in fifth.

The pronunciation /d/ occurs when the verb ends in a vowel or the sounds /b/, /d/, /g/, /dZ/ as in ridge, college, /l/, /m/, /n/,/N / (the sound represented by ng), /r/, /v/, /z/, and /D / as in breathe.

The pronunciation /Id/ occurs when the verb ends in –t or –d: waited, mended.

Examples

In English, the verb "to talk" is regular. This is not a particularly impressive feat in English, given that there are at most only five forms of each verb (apart from to be, which has eight), but it suffices.

Infinitive/ Present tense: "talk"

3rd person singular present tense: "talks"

Past tense: "talked"

Past participle: "talked"

Gerund/progressive (the present participle): "talking"

Compare with the verb "to think", an irregular verb.

Infinitive/Present tense: "think"

3rd person singular present tense: "thinks"

Past tense: "thought"

Past participle: "thought"

Gerund/progressive (the present participle): "thinking"

As a result, there are various ways of defining an irregular verb. A narrow definition will regard as irregular any verb which cannot be entirely deduced from a single form. This definition will allow that a language such as French may have more than one class of regular verb, provided the single learned form (in the case of French, the infinitive) shows by its inflection which class the verb belongs to; but where this is not the case, all deviations from the most frequent forms are irregular, yielding upwards of 900 irregular verbs in Latin, for example.

A less stringent definition will class verbs into types, which usually correspond roughly to historical categories, and treat as regular any verb which can be entirely deduced once one knows which category it belongs to. A looser definition still will regard as regular any verb which can be entirely deduced from a set of principal parts.

A psycholinguistic definition might lie somewhere in between, ignoring the paradigms as such and regarding as regular any verb which the native speaker's brain processes according to its rules. Since the brain works by analogy, minor groups may well be handled according to their rules, but much research is still required here.

Since the touchstone of these definitions is their usefulness in the classroom, there can be more than one valid approach, and we may wish to deal with different languages in different ways. For Old English, which has thousands of strong verbs which fit into a relatively small number of classes, it is usual to regard as regular any verb which can be deduced from its principal parts, but in textbooks for learners of modern English, a stricter definition of the regular verb is usual.

Causes of Irregularity

The most irregular verbs are suppletive, that is, their paradigm is made up of what were originally parts of different verbs. That this is inevitably irregular is obvious. An example is the verb 'to be' in most European languages. Another is English "to go", with its suppletive past tense "went".

Irregularity can be caused by a regular sound change in the history of a language which occurs only in certain phonetic environments and thus affects only parts of the verbal paradigm. An example is Grammatischer Wechsel, the consonant change between the forms was and were.

Irregularity can be caused by various forms of assimilation, which again may occur in only one part of a verb. An example is English think - thought, which displays both a vowel assimilation known as Rückumlaut and an entirely separate consonant assimilation known as the Germanic spirant law.

Irregularity can be caused by a shift of stress. For example, Latin verbs usually have their stress on the penultimate syllable. Since most present tense forms have a single-syllable inflection, this means the stress is on the stem, but the first and second persons plural have a two-syllable inflection, which meant the stress was on the inflection. In French a process of levelling means that stress is always on the stem. The vowel peculiarities typical of the nous and vous forms of French irregular verbs result from the fact that only these parts experienced a shift of stress: je peux, nous pouvons.

Sometimes a regular system may fall into relative disuse, so that its remnants are seen as irregular. An example is the Germanic strong verb, such as English speak.

Sometimes a perfect stem may come to be used as a present. (For example, the past tense of a verb meaning "to see" may come to be the present tense of a verb meaning "to know" - I know something if I have seen it.) The resulting verb then has past-tense inflections throughout its present tense, and may have gained a new (regular or irregular) past tense. Verbs of this sort in English are called preterite-presents; examples are can, may, must.

Almost all irregularities in verbs can be explained as part of the natural historical development of language, and grow out of some originally regular phenomenon.

Although the causes of irregular verbs are almost exclusively historical, the way we process them is a matter for synchronic linguistic studies, and in particular for psycholinguistics.

A common error for small children is to conjugate irregular verbs as though they were regular. This is regarded as evidence that we learn and process our native language partly by the application of rules, rather than, as some earlier scholarship had postulated, solely by learning the forms. In fact, children often use the most common irregular verbs correctly in their earliest utterances but then switch to incorrect regular forms for a time when they begin to operate systematically. This allows a fairly precise analysis of the phases of this aspect of first language acquisition.

IRREGULAR VERBS

The English language has a large number of irregular verbs. In the great majority of these, the past participle and/or past tense is not formed according to the usual patterns of English regular verbs. Other parts of the verb - such as the present 3rd person singular -s or -es, and present participle - ing - may still be formed regularly.

Among the exceptions are the verb to be and certain defective verbs which cannot be conjugated into certain tenses.

Most English irregular verbs are native, originating in Old English (an exception being 'catch'from Old North French 'cachier'.) They also tend to be the most commonly used verbs. The ten most commonly used verbs in English are all irregular.

Steven Pinker's book Words and Rules discusses how mistakes made by children in learning irregular verbs throw light on the mental processes involved in language acquisition.

All loanwords from foreign languages are regular. So are verbs that have been recently coined and all nouns used as verbs use standard suffixes. Almost all of the least commonly used words are also regular, even though some of them may have been irregular in the past.

Most irregular verbs exist as remnants of historical conjugation systems. What is today an exception actually followed a set, normal rule long ago. When that rule fell into disuse, some verbs kept the old conjugation. An example of this is the word kept, which before the Great Vowel Shift fell into a class of words where the vowel in keep (then pronounced kehp) was shortened in the past tense.

Similar words, such as peep, that arose after the Vowel Shift, use the regular -ed suffix. Groups of irregular verbs include:

— The remaining strong verbs, which display the vowel shift called ablaut and sometimes have a past participle in -en or -n: e.g., ride/rode/ridden. This verb group was inherited from the parent Proto-Germanic language, and ultimately from the Proto-Indo-European language, and was originally an entirely regular system. In Old English and in modern German it is still more or less regular, but in modern English the system of strong verb classes has almost entirely collapsed.

— Weak verbs that have been subjected to sound changes over the course of the history of English that have rendered them irregular. Many of these acquired a long vowel in the present stem, but kept a short vowel in the preterite and past participle; e.g., hear/heard/heard.

— Weak verbs that show the vowel shift are sometimes called "Rückumlaut"in the present tense e.g. think/thought.

— Weak verbs that end in a final -t or -d that made the addition of the weak suffix -ed seem redundant; e.g., cost/cost/cost.

— A handful of surviving preterite present verbs. These can be distinguished from the rest because their third person simple present singular (the he, she, or it form) does not take a final -s. These are the remnants of what was once a large Indo-European class of verbs that were conjugated in the preterite or perfect tense with present tense meaning. All of the surviving verbs of this class are modal verbs, that is, a class of auxiliary verbs or quasi-auxiliaries; e.g., can/could/could.

- Verbs that contain suppletive forms, which form one or more of their tenses from an entirely different root. Be is one of these, as is go/went/gone (where went is originally from the verb to wend). On the history of their paradigms, see: go (verb) and Indo-European copula.

Other verbs have been changed due to ease of pronunciation so that it is shorter or more closely corresponds to how it is spelt.

- A number of verbs whose irregularity is chiefly due to the peculiarities of English spelling; e.g., lay/laid/laid.
- Past tense ending -ed written phonetically when devoiced to -t; e.g., burn/burnt/burnt (which also has a regular conjugation with a [d] pronunciation).
- Weak verbs that have been the subject of contractions; e.g., have/had/had.

There are fewer strong verbs and irregular verbs in modern English than there were in Old English. Slowly over time, the number of irregular verbs is decreasing. The force of analogy tends to reduce the number of irregular verbs over time. This fact explains the reason that irregular verbs tend to be the most commonly used ones; verbs that are more rarely heard are more likely to switch to being regular. For instance, a verb like ablate was once irregular, but today ablated is the standard usage. Today irregular and standard forms often coexist, a sign that the irregular form may be on the wane. For instance, seeing spelled instead of spelt or strived instead of strove is very common. On the other hand, contraction and sound changes can increase their number. Most of the strong verbs were regular, in that they fell into a conventional plan of conjugation, in Old English; there are so few of them left in contemporary English that they seem irregular to us.

Common Irregularities

Common irregularities include:

Change the vowel to IPA: (the THOUGHT vowel), orthographically represented by ough or augh, e.g.

beseech → besought (now somewhat archaic; alternates with more recent regular form beseeched)

bring → brought

buy → bought

catch → caught

seek → sought

teach → taught

think → thought

— *Change the vowel to IPA:* (the GOAT vowel or "long O"), orthographically represented by o with a word-final e, e.g.

break → broke

choose → chose

freeze → froze

speak → spoke

steal → stole

To form past participle, add nasal suffix -en, e.g., broke → broken.

— *No change, e.g.,*

bet → bet

bid → bid

broadcast → broadcast

burst → burst

cast → cast

cost → cost

cut → cut

fit → fit (esp. U.S.)

hit → hit

hurt → hurt

knit → knit

let → let

put → put

quit → quit

rid → rid

set → set

shed → shed

shit → shit

shut → shut

spit → spit

split → split

spread → spread

sweat → sweat

thrust → thrust

wed → wed

wet → wet

More examples of irregular verbs are given below:

Base Form	Simple Past Tense	Past Participle
awake	awoke	awoken
be	was, were	been
bear	bore	born
beat	beat	beat
become	became	become
begin	began	begun
bend	bent	bent
beset	beset	beset
bet	bet	bet
bid	bid/bade	bid/bidden
bind	bound	bound
bite	bit	bitten
bleed	bled	bled
blow	blew	blown
break	broke	broken
breed	bred	bred
bring	brought	brought
broadcast	broadcast	broadcast
build	built	built
burn	burned/burnt	burned/burnt
burst	burst	burst
buy	bought	bought
cast	cast	cast
catch	caught	caught
choose	chose	chosen
cling	clung	clung
come	came	come
cost	cost	cost

creep	crept	crept
cut	cut	cut
deal	dealt	dealt
dig	dug	dug
dive	dived/dove	dived
do	did	done
draw	drew	drawn
dream	dreamed/dreamt	dreamed/dreamt
drive	drove	driven
drink	drank	drunk
eat	ate	eaten
fall	fell	fallen
feed	fed	fed
feel	felt	felt
fight	fought	fought
find	found	found
fit	fit	fit
flee	fled	fled
fling	flung	flung
fly	flew	flown
forbid	forbade	forbidden
forget	forgot	forgotten
forego (forgo)	forewent	foregone
forgive	forgave	forgiven
forsake	forsook	forsaken
freeze	froze	frozen
get	got	gotten
give	gave	given
go	went	gone

grind	ground	ground
grow	grew	grown
hang	hung	hung
hear	heard	heard
hide	hid	hidden
hit	hit	hit
hold	held	held
hurt	hurt	hurt
keep	kept	kept
kneel	knelt	knelt
knit	knit	knit
know	knew	know
lay	laid	laid
lead	led	led
leap	leaped/leapt	leaped/leapt
learn	learned/learnt	learned/learnt
leave	left	left
lendlent	lent	
let	let	let
lie	lay	lain
light	lighted/lit	lighted
lose	lost	lost
make	made	made
mean	meant	meant
meet	met	met
misspell	misspelled/ misspelt	misspelled/ misspelt
mistake	mistook	mistaken
mow	mowed	mowed/mown

overcome	overcame	overcome
overdo	overdid	overdone
overtake	overtook	overtaken
overthrow	overthrew	overthrown
pay	paid	paid
plead	pled	pled
prove	proved	proved/proven
put	put	put
quit	quit	quit
read	read	read
rid	rid	rid
ride	rode	ridden
ring	rang	rung
rise	rose	risen
run	ran	run
saw	sawed	sawed/sawn
say	said	said
see	saw	seen
seek	sought	sought
sell	sold	sold
send	sent	sent
set	set	set
sew	sewed	sewed/sewn
shake	shook	shaken
shave	shaved	shaved/shaven
shear	shore	shorn
shed	shed	shed
shine	shone	shone

shoe	shoed	shoed/shod
shoot	shot	shot
show	showed	showed/shown
shrink	shrank	shrunk
shut	shut	shut
sing	sang	sung
sink	sank	sunk
sit	sat	sat
sleep	slept	slept
slay	slew	slain
slide	slid	slid
sling	slung	slung
slit	slit	slit
smite	smote	smitten
sow	sowed	sowed/sown
speak	spoke	spoken
speed	sped	sped
spend	spent	spent
spill	spilled/spilt	spilled/spilt
spin	spun	spun
spit	spit/spat	spit
split	split	split
spread	spread	spread
spring	sprang/sprung	sprung
stand	stood	stood
steal	stole	stolen
stick	stuck	stuck
sting	stung	stung

stink	stank	stunk
stride	strod	stridden
strike	struck	struck
string	strung	strung
strive	strove	striven
swear	swore	sworn
sweep	swept	swept
swell	swelled	swelled/swollen
swim	swam	swum
swing	swung	swung
take	took	taken
teach	taught	taught
tear	tore	torn
tell	told	told
think	thought	thought
thrive	thrived/throve	thrived
throw	threw	thrown
thrust	thrust	thrust
tread	trod	trodden
understand	understood	understood
uphold	upheld	upheld
upset	upset	upset
wake	woke	woken
wear	wore	worn
weave	weaved/wove	weaved/woven
wed	wed	wed
weep	wept	wept
wind	wound	wound

win	won	won
withhold	withheld	withheld
withstand	withstood	withstood
wring	wrung	wrung
write	wrote	written

3

Tenses

English verbs, like those in many other western European languages, have more tenses than forms; tenses beyond the ones possible with the five forms listed above are formed with auxiliary verbs, as are the passive voice forms of these verbs. Important auxiliary verbs in English include will, used to form the future tense; shall, formerly used mainly for the future tense, but now used mainly for commands and directives; be, have, and do, which are used to form the supplementary tenses of the English verb, to add aspect to the actions they describe, or for negation.

English verbs display complex forms of negation. While simple negation was used well into the period of early Modern English in contemporary English negation almost always requires that the negative particle be attached to an auxiliary verb such as do or be. I go not is archaic; I do not go or I am not going are what the contemporary idiom requires.

English exhibits similar idiomatic complexity with the interrogative mood, which in Indo-

European languages is not, strictly speaking, a mood. Like many other Western European languages, English historically allowed questions to be asked by inverting the position of verb and subject: Whither goest thou? Now, in English, questions are often trickily idiomatic, and require the use of auxiliary verbs, though occasionally, the interrogative mood is still used in Modern English.

BASICS OF TENSES

In English grammar, tense refers to any conjugated form expressing time, aspect or mood. The large number of different composite verb forms means that English has the richest and subtlest system of tense and aspect of any Germanic language. This can be confusing for foreign learners; however, the English verb is in fact very systematic once one understands that in each of the three time spheres - past, present and future - English has a basic tense which can then be made either perfect or progressive (continuous) or both.

	Simple	Progressive	Perfect	Perfect progressive
Future	I will write	I will be writing	I will have written	I will have been writing
Present	I write	I am writing	I have written	I have been writing
Past	I wrote	I was writing	I had written	I had been writing

Because of the neatness of this system, modern textbooks on English generally use the terminology in this table. What was traditionally called the "perfect"is here called "present perfect"and the "pluperfect"becomes "past perfect", in order to show the relationships of the perfect forms to their respective simple forms. Whereas in other Germanic languages, or in Old English, the "perfect"is just a past tense, the English "present perfect"has a present reference; it is both a past tense and a present tense, describing the connection between a past event and a present state.

However, historical linguists sometimes prefer terminology which applies to all Germanic languages and is more helpful for comparative purposes; when describing wrote as a historical form, for example, we would say "preterite"rather than "past simple".

This table, of course, omits a number of forms which can be regarded as additional to the basic system:

- the intensive present I do write
- the intensive past I did write
- the habitual past I used to write
- the "shall future"I shall write
- the "going-to future"I am going to write
- the "future in the past"I was going to write
- the conditional I would write
- the perfect conditional I would have written
- the subjunctive, if I be writing, if I were writing.

Some systems of English grammar eliminate the future tense altogether, treating will/would simply as modal verbs, in the same category as other modal verbs such as can/could and may/might.

Present Smple Or Simple Present

— Affirmative: *I write; He writes*

— Negative: *He does not write*

— Interrogative: *Does he write ?*

— Negative interrogative: *Does he not write?*

Note that the "simple present"in idiomatic English often identifies habitual or customary action:

He writes about beavers (understanding that he does so all of the time.)

It is used with stative verbs:

She thinks that beavers are remarkable

It can also have a future meaning (though much less commonly than in many other languages):

She goes to Milwaukee on Tuesday.

Put Tuesday in the plural, and She goes to Milwaukee on Tuesdays means that she goes to Milwaukee every Tuesday.

The present simple has an intensive or emphatic form with "do": He does write. In the negative and interrogative forms, of course, this is identical to the non-emphatic forms. It is typically used as a response to the question Does he write, whether that question is expressed or implied, and says that indeed, he does write.

The different syntactic behavior of the negative particle not and the negative inflectional suffix -n't in the interrogative form is also worth noting. In formal literary English of the sort in which contractions are avoided, not attaches itself to the main verb: *Does he not write* ? When the colloquial contraction -n't is used, this attaches itself to the auxiliary do: *Doesn't he write* ? This in fact is a contraction of a more archaic word order, still occasionally found in poetry: *Does not he write*?

Present Progressive Or Present Continuous

- Affirmative: *He is writing*
- *Negative: He is not writing*
- Interrogative: *Is he writing*?
- Negative interrogative: *Is he not writing*?

This form describes the simple engagement in a present activity, with the focus on action in progress "at this very moment". It too can indicate a future, particularly when discussing plans already in place: *I am flying to Paris tomorrow*. Used with "always"it suggests irritation; compare *He always does that* (neutral) with *He is always doing that*. Word order differs here in the negative interrogative between the hyperformal is *he not writing and the usual isn't he writing?*

Present Perfect

Traditionally just called the perfect.

- Affirmative: *He has written*
- Negative: *He has not written*
- Interrogative: *Has he written*?
- Negative interrogative: *Has he not written*?

This indicates that a past event has one of a range of possible relationships to the present. This may be a focus on present result: *He has written a very fine book* (and look, here it is, we have it now). Or it may indicate a time-frame which includes the present. *I have lived here since my youth* (and I still do). Compare: *Have you written a letter this morning*? (it is still morning) with *Did you write a letter this morning*? (it is now afternoon). The perfect tenses are frequently used with the adverbs already or recently or with since clauses. Although the label "perfect tense"implies a completed action, the present perfect can identify habitual (I have written letters since I was ten years old.) or continuous (I have lived here for fifteen years.) action.

In addition to these normal uses where the time frame either is the present or includes the present, the "have done"construct is used in temporal clauses to define a future time: When you have written it, show it to me. It also forms a perfect infinitive, used when infinitive constructions require a past perspective: Mozart is said to have written his first symphony at the age of eight. (Notice that if not for the need of an infinitive, the simple past would have been used here: He wrote it at age eight.) The past infinitive is also used in the conditional perfect.

Present Perfect Progressive Or Continuous

— Affirmative: *He has been writing*

— Negative: *He has not been writing*

— Interrogative: *Has he been writing*?

— Negative interrogative: *Has he not been writing*?

Used for unbroken action in the past which continues right up to the present. *I have been writing this paper all morning* (and still am).

Present Perfect Continuous is used for denoting the action which was in progress and has just finished (a) or is still going on (b). For example,

a) *Why are your eyes red? - I have been crying since morning.* (The action has already finished but was in progress for some time)

b) *She has been working here for two years already and she is happy.* (The action is still in progress).

If we have to ask a question with "How long? "we should use the present perfect continuous. For example,

How long have you been working here ?

But with stative words (such as see, want, like, etc), or if the situation is considered permanent, we should use the present perfect simple. For example,

I have known her since childhood.

If we talk about the whole period of time, we use "for"and when we talk about the starting point of the action, we use "since".

We should not use the present simple tense for denoting actions that began in the past and are still going on. For example,

I am ill since Monday. (It is not correct).

I have been ill since Monday. (It is correct).

Past Simple

Or preterite. In older textbooks often called the imperfect.

— Affirmative: *He wrote*

— Negative: *He did not write*

— Interrogative: *Did he write* ?

— Negative interrogative: *Did he not write* ?

The same change of word order in the negative interrogative that distinguishes the formal and informal register also applies to the preterite. Note also that the preterite form is also used only in the affirmative. When the sentence is recast as a negative or interrogative, *he wrote not* and *wrote he*? are archaic and not used in modern English. They must instead be supplied by periphrastic forms. This tense is used for a single event in the past, sometimes for past habitual action, and in chronological narration. Like the present simple, it has emphatic forms with "do": he did write.

Although it is sometimes taught that the difference between the present perfect and the simple past is that the perfect denotes a completed action whereas the past denotes an incomplete action, this theory is clearly false. Both forms are normally used for completed actions. And either can be used for incomplete actions. The real distinction is that the present perfect is used when the time frame either is the present or includes the present, whereas the simple past is used when the time frame is in the absolute past.

The "used to"past tense for habitual actions is probably best included under the bracket of the past simple. Compare:

When I was young I played football every Saturday.

When I was young I used to play football every Saturday.

The difference is slight, but "used to"stresses the regularity, and the fact that the action has been discontinued.

Past Continuous or Imperfect or Past Progressive

— Affirmative: *He was writing*

— Negative: *He was not writing*

— Interrogative: *Was he writing*?

— Negative interrogative: *Was he not writing*?

This is typically used for two events in parallel:

While I was washing the dishes my wife was walking the dog.

Or for an interrupted action:

While I was washing the dishes I heard a loud noise.

Or when we are focusing on a point in the middle of a longer action:

At three o'clock yesterday I was working in the garden.

Past Perfect

Or the "pluperfect

— Affirmative: *He had written*

— Negative: *He had not written*

— Interrogative: *Had he written*?

— Negative interrogative: *Had he not written*?

Past Perfect Progressive Or Pluperfect Progressive or Continuous

— Affirmative: *He had been writing*

— Negative: *He had not been writing*

— Interrogative: *Had he been writing*?

— Negative interrogative: *Had he not been writing*?

Relates to the past perfect much as the present perfect progressive relates to the present perfect, but tends to be used with less precision.

Future Simple

— Affirmative: *He will write*

— Negative: *He will not write*

— Interrogative: *Will he write*?

— Negative interrogative: *Will he not write*?

There is also a future with "go" which is used especially for intended actions, and for the weather, and generally is more common in colloquial speech:

I am going to write a book some day.

I think that it is going to rain.

But the will future is preferred for spontaneous decisions:

Jack: "I think that we should have a barbecue!"

Jill: "Good idea! I shall go get the coal."

Future Progressive

— Affirmative: *He will be writing*

— Negative: *He will not be writing*

— Interrogative: *Will he be writing*?

— Negative interrogative: *Will he not be writing*?

Used especially to indicate that an event will be in progress at a particular point in the future: This time tomorrow I will be taking my driving test.

Future Perfect

- Affirmative: *He will have written*
- Negative: *He will not have written*
- Interrogative: *Will he have written?*
- Negative interrogative: *Will he not have written?*

Used for something which will be completed by a certain time (perfect in the literal sense) or which leads up to a point in the future which is being focused on.

I will have finished my essay by Thursday.

By then she will have been there for three weeks.

Future Perfect Progressive or Future Perfect Continuous

- Affirmative: *He will have been writing*
- Negative: *He will not have been writing*
- Interrogative: *Will he have been writing?*
- Negative interrogative: *Will he not have been writing?*

Conditional or Past Subjunctive.

- Affirmative: *He would write*
- Negative: *He would not write*
- Interrogative: *Would he write?*
- Negative interrogative: *Would he not write?*

Used principally in a main clause accompanied by an implicit or explicit doubt or "if-clause"; may refer to conditional statements in present or future time:

I would like to pay now if it is not too much trouble. (in present time; doubt of possibility is explicit)

I would like to pay now. (in present time; doubt is implicit)

I would do it if she asked me. (in future time; doubt is explicit)

I would do it. (in future time; doubt is implicit)

A very common error by foreign learners is to put the would into the if-clause itself. A humorous formulation of the rule for the EFL classroom runs: "If and would you never should, if and will makes teacher ill!"But of course, both will and would CAN occur in an if-clause when expressing volition. A student of English may rarely encounter the incorrect construction as it can occur as an archaic form.

Conditional Perfect or Pluperfect Subjunctive/Past-perfect Subjunctive.

— Affirmative: *He would have written*

— Negative: *He would not have written*

— Interrogative: *Would he have written?*

— Negative interrogative: *Would he not have written?*

Used as the past tense of the conditional form; expresses thoughts which are or may be contrary to present fact:

I would have set an extra place if I had known you were coming. (fact that an extra place was not set is implicit; conditional statement is explicit)

I would have set an extra place, but I did not because Mother said you were not coming. (fact that a place was not set is explicit; conditional is implicit)

I would have set an extra place. (fact that a place was not set is implicit, conditional is implicit)

Conditional Perfect Progressive

— Affirmative: *He would have been writing*

— Negative: *He would not have been writing*

— Interrogative: *Would he have been writing*?

— Negative interrogative: *Would he not have been writing?*

Present Subjunctive

The form is always identical to the infinitive. This means that, apart from the verb "to be", it is distinct only in the third person singular and the obsolete second person singular.

— Indicative: *I write, thou writest, he writes, I am*

— Subjunctive: *I write, thou write, he write, I be*

Used to refer to situations which are or may be contrary to fact in the present or future; the infactuality is rarely explicit:

I insist that he come at once. (present time; fact that the action is not currently occurring is implicit)

I insist that he come when I call. (future time; fact that the action may or may not occur is implicit)

(The present subjunctive is often interchangeable with the past subjunctive like so: *I insist that he must come at once.*)

Imperfect Subjunctive

The use of the old term "imperfect"shows that this form is so rare that it has not been integrated into the modern system of English tense classification. The imperfect subjunctive is identical to the past simple in every verb except the verb "to be". With this verb, there is an option, but no longer a necessity, of using were throughout all forms (i.e., *I wish I were an Oscar Meyer wiener*, vs. *I wish I was a girl)*.

— Indicative: *I was*

— Traditional Subjunctive: *I were*

— Colloquial Subjunctive: *I was*

— *If I were rich, I would retire to the South of France.*

4

Auxiliary Verb

An auxiliary (also called helping verb, helper verb, auxiliary verb, or verbal auxiliary) is a verb functioning to give further semantic or syntactic information about the main or full verb following it. In English, the extra meaning an auxiliary verb imparts alters the basic form of the main verb to have one or more of the following functions: passive, progressive, perfect, modal, or dummy.

In English, every clause has a finite verb which consists of a full verb (a non-auxiliary verb) and optionally one or more auxiliary verbs, each of which is a separate word. Examples of finite verbs include write (no auxiliary verb), have written (one auxiliary verb), and have been written (two auxiliary verbs).

There is a syntactic difference between an auxiliary verb and a full verb; that is, each has a different grammatical function within the sentence. In English, and in many other languages, there are some verbs that can act either as auxiliary or as full verbs, such as be ("I am writing a letter" vs "I am a postman") and have ("I have written a letter" vs "I have a letter"). In the case of be, it is sometimes ambiguous whether it is auxiliary or not; for example, "The ice cream was melted"could mean either "Someone/something melted the ice cream"(in which case melt would be the main verb) or "the ice cream was mostly liquid"(in which case be would be the main verb).

Helping verbs or auxiliary verbs such as will, shall, may, might, can, could, must, ought to, should, would, used to, need are used in conjunction with main verbs to express shades of time and mood. The combination of helping verbs with main verbs creates what are called verb phrases or verb strings. In the following sentence, "will have been"are helping or auxiliary verbs and "studying"is the main verb; the whole verb string is underlined:

As of next August, I *will have been studying* chemistry for ten years.

Students should remember that adverbs and contracted forms are not, technically, part of the verb. In the sentence, "He has already started."the adverb already modifies the verb, but it is not really part of the verb. The same is true of the 'nt in "He hasn't started yet"(the adverb not, represented by the contracted not, is not part of the verb, has started).

Shall, will and forms of have, do and be combine with main verbs to indicate time and voice. As auxiliaries, the verbs be, have and do can change form to indicate changes in subject and time.

— I *shall* go now.

— He *had* won the election.

- They *did* write that novel together.
- I *am* going now.
- He *was* winning the election.
- They *have been* writing that novel for a long time.

In England, shall is used to express the simple future for first person I and we, as in "Shall we meet by the river?" "Will would be used in the simple future for all other persons. Using will in the first person would express determination on the part of the speaker, as in "We will finish this project by tonight, by golly!" Using shall in second and third persons would indicate some kind of promise about the subject, as in "This shall be revealed to you in good time.} " This usage is certainly acceptable in the U.S., although shall is used far less frequently. The distinction between the two is often obscured by the contraction 'll, which is the same for both verbs.

In the United States, we seldom use shall for anything other than polite questions (suggesting an element of permission) in the first-person:

- "Shall we go now?"
- "Shall I call a doctor for you?"

(In the second sentence, many writers would use should instead, although should is somewhat more tentative than shall.) In the U.S., to express the future tense, the verb will is used in all other cases.

Shall is often used in formal situations (legal or legalistic documents, minutes to meetings, etc.) to express obligation, even with third-person and second-person constructions:

— The board of directors shall be responsible for payment to stockholders.

— The college president shall report financial shortfalls to the executive director each semester."

Should is usually replaced, nowadays, by would. It is still used, however, to mean "ought to"as in

— You really shouldn't do that.

— If you think that was amazing, you should have seen it last night.

In British English and very formal American English, one is apt to hear or read should with the first-person pronouns in expressions of liking such as "I should prefer iced tea"and in tentative expressions of opinion such as

— I should imagine they'll vote Conservative.

— I should have thought so.

Functions of the English Auxiliary Verb

Passive voice

The auxiliary verb be is used with a past participle to form the passive voice; for example, the clause "the door was opened"implies that someone (or something) opened it, without stating who (or what) it was. Because many past participles are also stative adjectives, the passive voice can sometimes be ambiguous; for example, "at 8:25, the window was closed"can be a passive-voice sentence meaning "at 8:25, someone closed the window,"or a non-passive-voice sentence meaning "at 8:25, the window was not open". Perhaps due to this ambiguity, the verb get will sometimes be used colloquially instead of be in forming the passive voice, "at 8:25, the window got closed".

Progressive Aspect

The auxiliary verb be is used with a present participle to form the progressive aspect; for example, the sentence "I am riding my bicycle"describes what the speaker is doing at the very moment of utterance, while the sentence "I ride my bicycle"is a temporally broader statement.

Perfect Aspect

The auxiliary verb have is used with a past participle to form the perfect aspect; for example, the sentence "Peter has fallen in love"differs from "Peter fell in love"in that the former implies some connection to the present - likely that Peter is still in love - while the latter does not.

Modal

There are nine modal verbs: can, could, may, might, shall, should, will, would, and must. They differ from the other auxiliaries both in that they are defective verbs, and in that they can never function as main verbs. (There do exist main verbs can and will, but these are distinct.) They express the speaker's (or listener's) judgement or opinion at the moment of speaking. Some of the modal verbs have been seen as a conditional tense form in English.

Some schools of thought consider could to represent the past tense of can. However, according to Michael Lewis (The English Verb), this is not always true. "Could I get you something?"clearly is not expressing past time. Lewis instead suggests that could is a remote form of can. It is evident after re-examining the usage of could in this light that remoteness does describe the general meaning, e.g.

— I couldn't do it. (remoteness of time)
— It could happen. (remoteness of possibility)
— Could you do me a favor? (remoteness of relationship)

The remaining modal auxiliaries can be viewed in this same manner.

Helping verbs, also called as modal auxiliaries or modals, such as can, could, may, might, must, ought to, shall, should, will, and would, do not change form for different subjects. For instance, try substituting any of these modal auxiliaries for can with any of the subjects listed below.

I you (singular) he we you (plural) they	can write well.

There is also a separate section on the Modal Auxiliaries, which divides these verbs into their various meanings of necessity, advice, ability, expectation, permission, possibility, etc., and provides sample sentences in various tenses.

The modal auxiliary *can* is used:

- to express ability (in the sense of .being able to do something or knowing how to do something): He can speak Spanish but he can't write it very well.
- to expression permission (in the sense of being allowed or permitted to do something):Can I talk to my friends in the library waiting room? (Note that can is less formal than may. Also, some writers will object to the use of can in this context.)
- to express theoretical possibility:American automobile makers can make better cars if they think there's a profit in it.

The modal auxiliary *could* is used

- to express an ability in the past:I could always beat you at tennis when we were kids.
- to express past or future permission:Could I bury my cat in your back yard?
- to express present possibility:We could always spend the afternoon just sitting around talking.
- to express possibility or ability in contingent circumstances:If he studied harder, he could pass this course.

In expressing ability, can and could frequently also imply willingness: Can you help me with my homework?

Can versus *May*:

Whether the auxiliary verb can can be used to express permission or not - "Can I leave the room now?"["I don't know if you can, but you may."] - depends on the level of formality of your text or situation. As Theodore Bernstein puts it in The Careful Writer, "a writer who is attentive to the proprieties will preserve the traditional distinction: can for ability or power to do something, may for permission to do it.

The question is at what level can you safely ignore the "proprieties."Merriam-Webster's Dictionary, tenth edition, says the battle is over and can can be used in virtually any situation to express or ask for permission. Most authorities, however, recommend a stricter adherence to the distinction, at least in formal situations.

Uses of *May* and *Might*:

Two of the more troublesome modal auxiliaries are may and might. When used in the context of granting or seeking permission, might is the past tense of may. Might is considerably more tentative than may.

— May I leave class early?

— If I've finished all my work and I'm really quiet, might I leave early?

In the context of expressing possibility, may and might are interchangeable present and future forms and might + have + past participle is the past form:

— She might be my advisor next semester.

— She may be my advisor next semester.

— She might have advised me not to take biology.

Avoid confusing the sense of possibility in may with the implication of might, that a hypothetical situation has not in fact occurred. For instance, let's say there's been a helicopter crash at the airport. In his initial report, before all the facts are gathered, a newscaster could say that the pilot "may have been injured." After we discover that the pilot is in fact all right, the newscaster can now say that the pilot "might have been injured" because it is a hypothetical situation that has not occurred. Another example: a body had been identified after much work by a detective. It was reported that "without this painstaking work, the body may have remained unidentified." Since the body was, in fact, identified, might is clearly called for.

Uses of *Will* and *Would*

In certain contexts, will and would are virtually interchangeable, but there are differences. Notice that the contracted form 'll is very frequently used for will. Will can be used to express willingness:

- I'll wash the dishes if you dry.
- We're going to the movies. Will you join us? It can also express intention (especially in the first person):
- I'll do my exercises later on. and prediction:
- specific: The meeting will be over soon.
- timeless: Humidity will ruin my hairdo.
- habitual: The river will overflow its banks every spring.

Would can also be used to express willingness:

- Would you please take off your hat? It can also express insistence (rather rare, and with a strong stress on the word "would"):

— Now you've ruined everything. You would act that way. and characteristic activity:

— customary: After work, he would walk to his home in West Hartford.

— typical (casual): She would cause the whole family to be late, every time. In a main clause, would can express a hypothetical meaning:

— My cocker spaniel would weigh a ton if I let her eat what she wants. Finally, would can express a sense of probability:

— I hear a whistle. That would be the five o'clock train.

Uses of *Used to*

The auxiliary verb construction used to is used to express an action that took place in the past, perhaps customarily, but now that action no longer customarily takes place:

— We used to take long vacation trips with the whole family. The spelling of this verb is a problem for some people because the "-ed"ending quite naturally disappears in speaking: "We yoostoo take long trips."But it ought not to disappear in writing. There are exceptions, though. When the auxiliary is combined with another auxiliary, did, the past tense is carried by the new auxiliary and the "-ed"ending is dropped. This will often happen in the interrogative:

— Didn't you use to go jogging every morning before breakfast?

– It didn't use to be that way. Used to can also be used to convey the sense of being accustomed to or familiar with something:

– The tire factory down the road really stinks, but we're used to it by now.

– I like these old sneakers; I'm used to them. Used to is best reserved for colloquial usage; it has no place in formal or academic text.

Dummy

Because, aside from the verbs to be and to have, only auxiliaries can be inverted to form questions and only auxiliaries can take negation directly, a dummy auxiliary do is used for questions and negatives when only a full verb exists in the positive statement (i.e. there are no auxiliaries in the positive, non-interrogative form). The same dummy do is used for emphasis in the positive statement form. This is known as do-insertion.

For example, if the positive statement form is:

– I know the way.

The interrogative, negative and emphatic forms are respectively:

– Do you know the way?

– I don't know the way.

– I do know the way.

Compare this with:

– I should know the way.

– Should I know the way?

– I shouldn't know the way.

Uses of Do, Does and Did

In the simple present tense, do will function as an auxiliary to express the negative and to ask questions. (Does, however, is substituted for third-person, singular subjects in the present tense. The past tense did works with all persons, singular and plural.)

— I don't study at night.

— She doesn't work here anymore.

— Do you attend this school?

— Does he work here?

These verbs also work as "short answers," with the main verb omitted.

— Does she work here? No, she doesn't work here.

With "yes-no" questions, the form of do goes in front of the subject and the main verb comes after the subject:

— Did your grandmother know Truman?

— Do wildflowers grow in your back yard?

Forms of do are useful in expressing similarity and differences in conjunction with so and neither.

— My wife hates spinach and so does my son.

— My wife doesn't like spinach; neither do I.

Do is also helpful because it means you don't have to repeat the verb:

— Larry excelled in language studies; so did his brother.

— Raoul studies as hard as his sister does.

The so-called emphatic do has many uses in English.

a. To add emphasis to an entire sentence: "He does like spinach. He really does!"

b. To add emphasis to an imperative: "Do come in."(actually softens the command)

c. To add emphasis to a frequency adverb: "He never did understand his father.""She always does manage to hurt her mother's feelings."

d. To contradict a negative statement: "You didn't do your homework, did you?""Oh, but I did finish it."

e. To ask a clarifying question about a previous negative statement: "Ridwell didn't take the tools.""Then who did take the tools?"

f. To indicate a strong concession: "Although the Clintons denied any wrong-doing, they did return some of the gifts."

In the absence of other modal auxiliaries, a form of do is used in question and negative constructions known as the get passive:

- Did Rinaldo get selected by the committee?
- The audience didn't get riled up by the politician.

Uses of Have, Has and Had

Forms of the verb to have are used to create tenses known as the present perfect and past perfect. The perfect tenses indicate that something has happened in the past; the present perfect indicating that something happened and might be continuing to happen, the past perfect indicating that something happened prior to something else happening.

To have is also in combination with other modal verbs to express probability and possibility in the past.

— As an affirmative statement, to have can express how certain you are that something happened (when combined with an appropriate modal + have + a past participle): "Georgia must have left already.""Clinton might have known about the gifts.""They may have voted already."

— As a negative statement, a modal is combined with not + have + a past participle to express how certain you are that something did not happen: "Clinton might not have known about the gifts.""I may not have been there at the time of the crime."

— To ask about possibility or probability in the past, a modal is combined with the subject + have + past participle: "Could Clinton have known about the gifts?"

— For short answers, a modal is combined with have: "Did Clinton know about this?""I don't know. He may have.""The evidence is pretty positive. He must have."

To have (sometimes combined with to get) is used to express a logical inference:

— It's been raining all week; the basement has to be flooded by now.

— He hit his head on the doorway. He has got to be over seven feet tall!

Have is often combined with an infinitive to form an auxiliary whose meaning is similar to "must."

— I have to have a car like that!

— She has to pay her own tuition at college.

— He has to have been the first student to try that.

QUASI-AUXILIARIES

English contains many verb phrases that function as quasi-auxiliaries, such as be going to, used to, is about to. These quasi-auxiliaries require an infinitive. Others take a gerund, past participle or other verb form.

In American English, go and come can be quasi-auxiliaries with nothing between them and the following verb phrases, but only in their plain forms: "Come show me", "I'll go get it", and "I had to come see for myself". This use can be regarded as ellipsis of and - the previous are equivalent to "Come and show me", "I'll go and get it", and "I had to come and see for myself"- and British English requires the and to be included, as does American English when the verb is not in its plain form: "I went and saw him."

PROPERTIES OF THE ENGLISH AUXILIARY VERB

Negation

Auxiliaries take not (or n't) to form the negative, e.g. can't, won't, shouldn't, etc. In certain tenses, in questions, when a contracted auxiliary verb can be used, the position of the negative particle n't moves from the main verb to the auxiliary: cf. Does it not work? and Doesn't it work?

Inversion

Auxiliaries invert to form questions:

— You will come.

— Will you come?

Emphasis

The dummy auxiliary do is used for emphasis in positive statements:

— I do like this beer!

Ellipsis

Auxiliaries can appear alone where a main verb has been omitted, but is understood:

— I will go, but she won't [go].

The verb do can act as a pro-VP (or occasionally a pro-verb) to avoid repetition:

— John never sings in the kitchen, but Mary does.

— John never sings in the kitchen, but Mary does in the shower. (pro-verb: replaces sings)

Tag Questions

Auxiliaries can be repeated at the end of a sentence, with negation added or removed, to form a tag question. In the event that the sentence did not use an auxiliary verb, a dummy auxiliary (a form of do) is used instead:

— You will come, won't you?

— You ate, didn't you?

— You won't come, will you?

— You didn't eat, did you?

5

Compound Verb

A compound verb or complex predicate is a multi-word compound that acts as a single verb. One component of the compound is a light verb or vector, which carries any inflections, indicating tense, mood, or aspect, but provides only fine shades of meaning. The other, "primary", component is a verb or noun which carries most of the semantics of the compound, and determines its arguments. It is usually in either base or conjunctive participial form.

A compound verb is also called a "complex predicate"because the semantics, as formally modeled by a predicate, is determined by the primary verb, though both verbs appear in the surface form. Whether Noun+Verb (N+V) compounds are considered to be "compound verbs"is a matter of naming convention. Generally, the term complex predicate usually includes N+V compounds, whereas the term compound verb is usually reserved for V+V compounds. However, several authors also refer to N+V compounds as compound verbs.

Compound verbs are to be distinguished from serial verbs which typically signify a sequence of actions, and in which the verbs are relatively equal in semantic and grammatical weight.

STRUCTURE

Thus, there are two classes of complex predicates:

1. *V+V compounds:* The true compound verb, where the first verb is a Light verb (LV), followed by a primary or Heavy verb. With a few exceptions all compound verbs alternate with their simple counterparts.
2. *N+V compounds*: A compound with Noun+verb, converting the noun into a verbal structure; the arguments and the semantics are determined by the N and the tense markers / inflections are carried by the V. This would include English stretched verb examples like take a walk or commit suicide. Often the Verbs participating N+V compounding are also those that participate as LVs in V+V compounds. The N+V compound appears in almost all languages, especially with LVs such as "do", "make"etc., and are sometimes not considered to be a true compound verb.

Compound verbs are very common in all the languages of India, though they are more frequent in the northern Indo-Aryan languages than in Dravidian languages. In addition to Hindi-Urdu and Panjabi, they occur in other Indo-Iranian languages like Persian, Marathi and Nepali, in Tibeto-Burman languages like Limbu and Newari. Also, they are very frequent in Altaic languages like Korean,

Japanese, and in Central Asian Indo-European languages.

Conventionally, the English language expresses fine distinctions as to the beginning, duration, completion, or repetition, of an action in the form of compound verbs, using auxiliaries or other lexical mechanisms. Examples here include was starting, had lived, had been seen, etc. This usage reduced the need to create complex predicates.

Though V+V compound verbs are rare in English, one may illustrate the form with the example "start reading". In some interpretations, one may consider "start"as a light verb, which carries markers like tense. However, the main part of the meaning, as well as the arguments of "started reading", i.e. answers to questions such as who→ (agent), or what was it that he "started reading"(object) are determined by the second, primary verb, "read". Note that "start"also modifies the meaning or the semantics, by focusing on the early part of the "reading". Also note that "start"carries plural/tense markers, whereas "reading"appears in this fixed form, and does not change with tense, number, gender etc.

Whether gerundive forms like "start reading"are compound verbs or not is controversial in English; many linguists prefer to treat "reading"treated as a nominal in its gerundive form. However, the compound verb treatment may have some advantages, particularly when it comes to semantic analysis. For example, in X starts reading Y, the question what did X start is less revealing than what did x "start reading".

Compound verb is usually composed of a preposition and a verb, although other combinations also exist. From a morphological point of view, some compound verbs are difficult to analyze because several derivations are plausible. Blacklist, for instance, might be analyzed as an adjective+verb compound, or as an adjective+noun compound that becomes a verb through zero derivation. Most compound verbs originally have the collective meaning of both components, but some of them later gain additional meanings that may predominate the original, accurate sense. Therefore, sometimes the resultant meanings are seemingly barely related to the original contributors.

Compound verbs composed of a noun and verb are comparatively rare, and the noun is generally not the direct object of the verb. In English, compounds such as *bread-bake or *car-drive do not exist. Yet, we find literal action words, such as breastfeed, taperecord and washing instructions on clothing as for example hand wash.

Compound verbs with single-syllable modifiers are solid, or unhyphenated. Those with longer modifiers may originally be hyphenated, but as they became established, they became solid, e.g.,

— overhang (English origin)
— counterattack (Latin origin)

There was a tendency in the 18th century to use hyphens excessively, that is, to hyphenate all previously established solid compound verbs. American English, however, has diminished the use of hyphens, while British English is more conservative

6

Phrasal Verbs

A phrasal verb is a combination of a verb and preposition, a verb and adverb, or a verb with both an adverb and preposition, any of which are part of the syntax (of the sentence), and so are a complete semantic unit. Its sentences may, however, contain direct and indirect objects in addition to the phrasal verb. Phrasal verbs are particularly frequent in the English language. A phrasal verb often has a meaning which is different from the original verb.

According to Tom McArthur: .the term 'phrasal verb'was first used by Logan Pearsall Smith, in "Words and Idioms", in which he states that the OED Editor Henry Bradley suggested the term to him.

Alternative terms for phrasal verb are 'compound verb', 'verb-adverb combination', 'verb-particle construction (VPC)', AmE "two-part word/ verb'and 'three-part word/verb' and multi-word verb (MWV).'Preposition' and 'adverb'as used in a phrasal verb are also called 'particle'in that they do not alter their form through inflections (are therefore uninflected, they do not accept affixes, etc.).

Phrasal verbs are usually used informally in everyday speech as opposed to the more formal Latinate verbs, such as "to get together"rather than "to congregate", "to put off"rather than "to postpone", or "to get out"rather than "to exit".

Many verbs in English can be combined with an adverb or a preposition, and readers or listeners will easily understand a phrasal verb used in a literal sense with a preposition:

— "He walked across the square."

Verb and adverb constructions can also easily be understood when used literally:

— "She opened the shutters and looked outside."

— "When he heard the crash, he looked up."

An adverb in a literal phrasal verb modifies the verb it is attached to, and a preposition links the subject to the verb.

It is, however, the figurative or idiomatic application in everyday speech which makes phrasal verbs so important:

— "I hope you will get over your operation quickly."

— "Work hard, and get your examination over."

The literal meaning of "to get over", in the sense of "to climb over something to get to the other side", no longer applies to explain the subject's enduring an operation or the stress of an examination which they have to overcome. It is when the combined meaning of verb plus adverb, or verb plus preposition is totally different from each its component parts, that the semantic content of the phrasal verb cannot be predicted by its constituent parts and so becomes much more difficult for a student learning English to recognise.

Other idiomatic usages of phrasal verbs show a verb + direct object + preposition/adverb + indirect object construction:

In her introduction to "Longman Dictionary of Phrasal Verbs, What this dictionary contains", Rosemary Courtney includes as a third category.

Idioms which are formed from phrasal verbs, such as let the cat out of the bag. These idioms are printed in heavy type. Idioms have a meaning which is different from the meaning of the single words, and usually have a fixed word order.

Courtney then cites among many other examples in the dictionary such phrases as "to add insult to injury", "to add fuel to the flames", "to leave someone in the lurch", "to scare someone out of their wits", etc.

PHRASAL VERB PATTERNS

A phrasal verb contains either a preposition or an adverb (or both), and may also combine with one or more nouns or pronouns.

Particle Verbs

Phrasal verbs that contain adverbs are sometimes called "particle verbs", and are related to separable verbs in other Germanic languages. There are two main patterns: intransitive and transitive. An intransitive particle verb does not have an object:

— "When I entered the room he looked up."

A transitive particle verb has a nominal object in addition to the adverb. If the object is an ordinary noun, it can usually appear on either side of the adverb, although very long noun phrases tend to come after the adverb:

— Switch off the light.

— Switch the light off.

— Switch off the lights in the hallway next to the bedroom the president is sleeping in.

With some transitive particle verbs, however, the noun object must come after the adverb. Such examples are said to involve "inseparable"phrasal verbs:

— The gas gave off fumes. (not *The gas gave fumes off.)

Still other transitive particle verbs require the object to precede the adverb:

— They let the man through. (not *They let through the man.)

With all transitive particle verbs, if the object is a pronoun, it must normally precede the adverb:

— Switch it off. (not *Switch off it.)

— The gas gave them off. (not *gave off them)

— They let him through. (not *let through him)

Prepositional Verbs

Prepositional verbs are phrasal verbs that contain a preposition, which is always followed by its nominal object. They are different from inseparable transitive particle verbs, because the object still follows the preposition if it is a pronoun:

— On Fridays, we look after our grandchildren.

— We look after them. (not *look them after)

The verb can have its own object, which usually precedes the preposition:

— She helped the boy to an extra portion of potatoes.

— with pronouns: She helped him to some.

Prepositional verbs with two prepositions are possible:

— We talked to the minister about the crisis.

Phrasal-prepositional Verbs

A phrasal verb can contain an adverb and a preposition at the same time. Again, the verb itself can have a direct object:

— no direct object: The driver got off to a flying start.

— direct object: Onlookers put the accident down to the driver's loss of concentration.

Phrasal Verbs and Modifying Adverbs

When modifying adverbs are used alongside particle adverbs intransitively (as particle adverbs usually are), the adverbs can appear in any verb/particle/adverb positions:

— "He unhappily looked round."

— "He looked unhappily round."

— "He looked round unhappily."

The particle adverb here is "round"and the modifying adverb is "unhappily". ("Round"is a particle because it is not inflected - does not take affixes and alter its form. "Unhappily"is a modifying adverb because it modifies the verb "look").

With a transitive particle verb, the adverb goes either before the verb of after the object or particle, whichever is last:

— "He cheerfully picked the book up."

— "He picked up the book cheerfully."(not *picked cheerfully up the book)

— "He picked the book up cheerfully."

Prepositional verbs are different from transitive particle verbs, because they allow adverbs to appear between the verb and the preposition:

— "He cheerfully looked after the children.

— "He looked after the children cheerfully.

— "He looked cheerfully after the children.

Phrasal Verbs Combined with Special Verb Forms and Clauses

Rosemary Courtney also includes special verb forms and clauses in phrasal verb constructions.

Phrasal verbs combined with wh-clauses and that-clauses:

Sentences which include verb + particle + object(s) + wh-clauses:

— "The teacher tried to dictate to his class what is the right thing to do"

= transitive verb + preposition(dictate to) + direct object (his class) + wh-clause (what is the right thing to do).

— "My friends called for me when the time came"

= transitive verb + preposition (called for) + pronoun (me) + wh-clause (when the time came).

— "Watch out that you don't hit your head on the low beam"

= intransitive verb + adverb (watch out) + that-clause (that you don't hit your head on the low beam).

Phrasal Verbs Combined with Verb-ing Forms

— "You can't prevent me from seeing her"

= transitive verb + pronoun (prevent me) + preposition (from) + verb-ing form (seeing) + pronoun (her).

TWO-PART (PHRASAL) VERBS (IDIOMS)

Many verbs in English are followed by an adverb or a preposition (also called a particle), and these two-part verbs, also called phrasal verbs, are different from verbs with helpers. The particle that follows the verb changes the meaning of the phrasal verb in idiomatic ways:

— *drop off* - decline gradually.

The hill dropped off near the river

— *drop off(2)* - fall asleep

While doing his homework, he dropped off.

— *drop off(3)* - stop and give something to someone

Would you drop this off at the post office

— *drop out* - cease to participate

After two laps, the runner dropped out.

Some particles can be separated from the verb so that a noun and pronoun can be inserted, and some particles can't be separated from the verb. In addition, some phrases are intransitive, meaning they cannot take a direct object.

— *Separable*

add up (meaning: to add)

Correct: She added up the total on her calculator.

Correct: She added it up on her calculator.

— *Inseparable*

get around (meaning: to evade)

Correct: She always gets around the rules.

Incorrect: She always gets the rules around (This construction makes no sense in English.)

— *Intransitive*

catch on (meaning: to understand)

Incorrect: She began to catch on the math problem. (catch on cannot take a direct object in this meaning.)

Correct: She began to catch on to the math problem. (the word to makes the math problem an indirect object, which is acceptable in this meaning.)

Unfortunately, there is usually no indicator whether an idiomatic phrase is separable, inseparable, or intransitive. In most cases the phrases must simply be memorized. Below is a partial list of each kind of phrase.

COMMON PHRASAL VERBS IN EXAMPLES

We often use verbs with these words:

on	off	in	out	up	down	away	
back	over	about	round	forward		through	along

We often use these words (particles) with verbs of *movements*. For example:

- *get on*. The bus was full. We couldn't get on.
- *drive off*. She got into the car and drove off.
- *came back*. Tom is leaving tomorrow and coming back on Saturday.
- *turn round*. When I touched him on the shoulder, he turned round.

But often these words (*on / off / up / down* etc.) give a special (an idiomatic) meaning to a verb. For example:

- Sorry I'm late. The car *broke down*.
- *Look out*! There's car coming.
- It was my first flight. I was very nervous as the plane *took off*.
- It was so tired this morning that I couldn't *get up*.
- How did you *get on* in your examination yesterday?

These multi-word verbs (*break down / get up / get on* etc.) are *phrasal verbs.*

Sometimes a multi-word verb has an *object*. Usually there are *two possible positions* for the object (noun or pronoun): before the particle or after the particle.

In general there are four types of multi-word verbs:

— Type1: Verb + particle (no object)

Intransitive Multi-Word Verbs

— Type2: Verb + particle + object

Separable Multi-Word Verbs

The object (noun or pronoun) can come between the verb and the particle.

But if the object is a pronoun, it *always* comes between the verb and the particle.

— Type3: Verb + particle + object

Inseparable Multi-Word Verbs (Transitive)

The object (noun or pronoun) *always* comes after the particle.

— Type4: Verb + particle + particle

Three-Word Phrasal Verbs (Transitive)

— Type 4 multi-word verbs are nearly always idiomatic. The object cannot change position. It cannot come before the particles, or between the particles.

Intransitive Phrasal Verbs: Examples

The following phrasal verbs are not followed by an

object: "Once you leave home, you can never really *go back* again."

- That old Jeep had a tendency to *break down* just when I needed it the most.
- Popular songs seem to *catch on* in California first and then spread eastward.
- Father promised that we would never *come back* to this horrible place.
- They tried to *come in* through the back door, but it was locked.
- He was hit on the head very hard, but after several minutes, he started to *come to* again.
- The children promised to *come over*, but they never do.
- We used to just *drop by*, but they were never home, so we stopped doing that.
- When we visited Paris, we loved *eating out* in the sidewalk cafes.
- Uncle Heine didn't have much money, but he always seemed to *get by* without borrowing money from relatives.
- Grandmother tried to *get up*, but the couch was too low, and she couldn't make it on her own.
- It's hard to imagine that we will ever *go back* to Lithuania.
- We would finish one Dickens novel and then just *go on* to the next.
- The cops heard all the noise and stopped to see what was *going on*.

— Charles *grew up* to be a lot like his father.

— The judge warned the stalker to *keep away* from his victim's home.

— He tried to *keep on singing* long after his voice was ruined.

— He had drunk too much; he *passed out* on the sidewalk outside the bar.

— Whenever he sat down at the piano, we knew he was going to *show off*.

— Day after day, Efrain *showed up* for class twenty minutes late.

— I *woke up* when the rooster crowed.

Separable Phrasal Verbs: Examples

The object may come after the following phrasal verbs or it may separate the two parts:

— I *turned off* the light.

— I *turned* the light *off*.

— You have to *do* this paint job *over*.

When the object of the following phrasal verb is a pronoun (*it / them / me / you / him / her / us*), the two parts of the phrasal verb must be separated: I *turned* it *off*.

— The terrorists tried to *blow up* the railroad station.

— The matter *brought up* at the committee.

— They *called off* this afternoon's meeting.

— Do *this homework* over.

— Fill out *this application form and mail it in.*

- She *filled up* the grocery cart with free food.
- My sister *found out* that her husband had been planning a surprise party for her.
- The filling station was *giving away* free gas.
- My brother borrowed my car. I have a feeling he's not about to *give* it *back*.
- The students *handed in* their papers and left the room.
- She *hung up* the phone before she *hung up* her clothes.
- I hate to *hold up* the meeting, but I have to go to the bathroom.
- Three masked gunmen *held up* the Security Bank this afternoon.
- You *left out* the part about the police chase down Asylum Avenue.
- The lawyers *looked over* the papers carefully before questioning the witness. They *looked* them *over* carefully.
- You've misspelled this word again. You'd better *look* it *up*.
- She knew she was in trouble, so she *made up* a story about going to the movies with her friends.

- He was so far away, we really couldn't *make out* what he was saying.
- There were three men in the line-up. She *picked out* the guy she thought had stolen her purse.
- The crane *picked up* the entire house. Watch them *pick* it *up*

— As we drove through Paris, Francoise *pointed out* the major historical sites.

— We *put away* money for our retirement. She *put away* the cereal boxes.

— We asked the boss to *put off* the meeting until tomorrow. (Please *put* it *off* for another day.)

— I *put on* a sweater and a jacket. (I *put* them *on* quickly.)

— The firefighters *put out* the house fire before it could spread. (They *put* it *out* quickly.)

— I *read over* the homework, but couldn't make any sense of it .

— My wife *set up* the living room exactly the way she wanted it. She *set* it *up*.

— These are your instructions. *Take* them *down* before you forget.

— It was so hot that I had to *take off* my shirt.

— We have serious problems here. Let's *talk* them *over* like adults.

— That's a lot of money! Don't just *throw* it *away*.

— She *tried on* fifteen dresses before she found one she liked.

— I *tried out* four cars before I could find one that pleased me.

— Your radio is driving me crazy! Please *turn* it*down*.

— He applied for a promotion twice this year, but he was *turned down* both times.

— Grandpa couldn't hear, so he *turned up* his hearing aid.

— We *turned off* the lights before anyone could see us.

— It was a disgusting movie. It really *turned* me *off.*

— Turn on *the CD player so we can dance.*

— The gang members *used up* all the money and went out to rob some more banks.

Inseparable Phrasal Verbs (Transitive)

With the following phrasal verbs, the lexical part of the verb (the part of the phrasal verb that carries the "verb-meaning") cannot be separated from the prepositions (or other parts) that accompany it: "Who will *look after* my estate when I'm gone?"

— The teacher *called on* students in the back row.

— The old minister continued to *call on* his sick parishioners.

— I *got over* the flu, but I don't know if I'll ever *get over* my broken heart.

— The students *went over* the material before the exam. They should have *gone over* it twice.

— They country *went through* most of its coal reserves in one year. Did he *go through* all his money already?

— My mother promised to *look after* my dog while I was gone.

— The police will *look into* the possibilities of embezzlement.

— I *ran across* my old roommate at the college reunion.

— Carlos *ran into* his English professor in the hallway.

— My second son seems to *take after* his mother.
— It seemed strange to see my old boss *wait on* tables.

Three-Word Phrasal Verbs (Transitive)

With the following phrasal verbs, you will find three parts: "My brother *dropped out of* school before he could graduate."

— I was talking to Mom on the phone when the operator *broke in on* our call.
— After our month-long trip, it was time to *catch up with* the neighbors and the news around town.
— I was talking to Mom on the phone when the operator *broke in on* our call.
— The boys promised to *check up on* the conditions of the summer house from time to time.
— After years of giving nothing, the old parishioner was able to *come up with* a thousand-dollar donation.
— We tried to *cut down on* the money we were spending on entertainment.
— I hope none of my students *drop out of* school this semester.
— I found it very hard to *get along with* my brother when we were young.
— Janik cheated on the exam and then tried to *get away with* it.
— The citizens tried to *get rid of* their corrupt mayor in the recent election.
— When will you ever *get through with* that program?

— It's hard to *keep up with* the Joneses when you lose your job!
— I always *look forward to* the beginning of a new semester.
— It's typical of a jingoistic country that the citizens *look down on* their geographical neighbors.
— We were going to *look in on* my brother-in-low, but he wasn't home.
— Good instructors will *look out for* early signs of failure in their students.
— First-graders really *look up to* their teachers.
— Make sure of *the student's identity before you let him into the classroom.*
— The teacher had to *put up with* a great deal of nonsense from new students.
— The runners *ran out of* energy before the end of the race.
— My oldest sister *took care of* us younger children after Mom died.
— The star player *talked back to* the coach and was thrown off the team.
— I often *think back on* my childhood with great pleasure.
— Her husband *walked out on* her and their three children.

Phrasal Verbs: One Verb After Another

Phrasal Verb: Look

— Are you still *looking [about] for* a job?

— Who will *look after* the baby.
— Look at *this picture, please.*
— He *looks at* work in a different way now he's in charge.
— They *look* carefully *at* a problem.
— Look at *Mrs Jones; drink killed her.*
— Something you were *looking for,* but you can't find it, and you can't remember what it was. So I'll tell you. It's the monitor you're *looking for,* and it isn't there.
— I'll *look in* and see you next week.
— Look out! *There is a car coming.*
— I half-expected Candy to open my door and *look out* to see what the fracas was, but the door stayed firmly closed.
— If you don't know the word *look* it *up* in the dictionary.

Phrasal Verb: Put

— Close the books and *put* them *aside*.
— I'll just *put* the car *away*.
— Take your notebooks and *put down* all the words that are on the board.
— Mr. Gough *put off* his trip to London until next month.
— She *put* her hat and coat *on*.
— She *put* the light [the fire] *out*.
— I can't *put up with* your rudeness anymore; leave the room.

Phrasal Verb: Come

— I *came across* this book in a little store.

— I want you *come along* (with us), or you'll miss the bus.

— Come back *here. I want to talk to you.*

— The button has *come off* my coat.

— Come on *or will be late.*

Phrasal Verb: Get

— They do *get along* (well) together.

— I am *getting off* at the next station (stop).

— How do you *get on*?

— It was too hard for her to *get over* that illness.

— Let's *get together.*

— If he *gets up* early, he'll come on time.

Phrasal Verb: Find

— She's unpleasant. She always *finds fault with* people.

— He *found himself* after graduating the University.

— You can't trust him until you *find* everything *out.*

Phrasal Verb: Run

— Yesterday I *ran into* my friend whom I haven't seen since we left school.

— Why are you so upset? - My kitten was *run over* by a car.

— I'll have to go to the baker's as we've *run out of* bread.

Phrasal Verb: Give

— They *gave away* their food for free.

— He has *given in* to my views.

— Give out *the textbooks.*

— He had to *give up* studying because of poor health.

— You should *give up* smoking.

Phrasal Verb: Go

— I don't *go in for* sport.

— The light *went off* and the film began.

— Go on *with your work.*

— You may take this book. I can easily *go without* it for a month.

Phrasal Verb: Turn

— Turn *that radio* down *at once.*

— My umbrella *turned inside out.*

— When leaving, don't forgot to *turn off* the stove.

— She *turns on* her charm whenever she wants anything.

— You'll have to *turn up* tomorrow. It's very important for us.

7

Transitive and Intransitive Verbs

In linguistics, transitivity is a property of verbs that relates to whether a verb can take direct objects. It is closely related to valency. Traditional grammar makes a binary distinction between transitive verbs such as throw, injure, kiss that take a direct object, versus intransitive verbs such as fall or sit that cannot take a direct object. In practice, many languages, such as English intepret the category more flexibly; allowing, for example, ambitransitive verbs or ditransitive verbs.In functional grammar, transitivity is considered to be a continuum rather than a binary category.

Transitive verbs are verbs that have subjects or objects that receive the action. They are either active voice or passive voice. Transitive active verbs are the verbs in sentences with a direct object. Example: The boy kicked the ball. The subject is the doer and the direct object is the receiver of the action. Transitive passive verbs have the subject receiving the action with the doer in a prepositional phrase or omitted in the sentence. Examples: The ball was kicked by the boy. The ball was kicked hard. The verb in the transitive passive voice always has is, am, are, was, were, be, being, or been as an auxiliary or helping verb.

Transitive active sentences can be changed to transitive passive sentences by making the direct object the subject and putting the subject either in a prepositional phrase or omitting it. Example: The daughter kissed her mother on the cheek. The mother was kissed on the cheek by her daughter. The mother was kissed on the cheek. (Mother is the receiver of the action in all three sentences, but in the last two sentences mother is the subject of the sentences.)

Many languages, such as Hungarian, mark transitivity through morphology; transitive verbs and intransitive verbs behave in distinctive ways. In languages with polypersonal agreement, an intransitive verb will agree with its subject only, while a transitive verb will agree with both subject and direct object.

In other languages the distinction is based on syntax. It is possible to identify an intransitive verb in English, for example, by attempting to supply it with an appropriate direct object:

— You kissed my hand - transitive verb.

— She injured him - transitive verb.

— What did you throw? - transitive verb.

By contrast, an intransitive verb coupled with a direct object will result in an ungrammatical utterance:

— What did you fall?

— I sat a chair.

Conversely (at least in a traditional analysis), using a transitive verb in English without a direct object will result in an incomplete sentence:

— I kissed (. . .)

— You injured (. . .)

— Where is she now? She's injuring.

English is unusually lax by Indo-European standards in its rules on transitivity; what may appear to be a transitive verb can be used as an intransitive verb, and vice versa. Eat and read and many other verbs can be used either transitively or intransitively. Often there is a semantic difference between the intransitive and transitive forms of a verb: the water is boiling versus I boiled the water; the grapes grew versus I grew the grapes. In these examples, the role of the subject differs between intransitive and transitive verbs.

Even though an intransitive verb may not take a direct object, it often may take an appropriate indirect object:

— I laughed at him.

What are considered to be intransitive verbs can also take cognate objects—where the object is considered integral to the action, for example I slept an hour.

INTRANSITIVE VERB

"Intransitive" redirects here. For intransitive relations in mathematics, see Intransitivity. In grammar, an intransitive verb does not take an object. In more technical terms, an intransitive verb has only one argument (its subject), and hence has a valency of one. For example, in English, the verbs sleep, complain and die, are intransitive.

Some examples of sentences with intransitive verbs:

— Harry will sleep until sunrise. (sleep has no object)

— You complain too much. (complain has no object)

— I die Friday. (die has no object)

In languages where a passive voice exists, a transitive verb can be passivized in order to turn it into an intransitive one. For example, the transitive verb hug becomes the intransitive verb phrase be hugged. Passivization involves deleting the subject and replacing it by the direct object (this shift is called promotion of the object).

Intransitive verbs, of course, cannot be passivized in the strict sense, However, some languages (like Dutch) have so-called impersonal passives that allow one to transform, e. g. He phoned

In many languages, there are ambitransitive verbs, which can be either transitive or intransitive. For example, English play is ambitransitive (both intransitive and transitive), since it is grammatical to say His son plays, and it is also grammatical to say His son plays guitar. English is rather flexible with regards to verb valency, and so it has a high number of ambitransitive verbs; other languages are more rigid and require explicit valency changing operations (voice, causative morphology, etc.) to transform a verb from intransitive to transitive or vice versa.

In some ambitransitive verbs, called ergative verbs, the alignment of the syntactic arguments to the semantic roles is exchanged. An example of this is the verb break in English.

(1) I broke the cup.

(2) The cup broke.

In (1), the verb is transitive, and the subject is the agent of the action, i. e. the performer of the action of breaking the cup. In (2), the verb is intransitive and the subject is the patient of the action, i. e. it is the thing affected by the action, not the one that performs it. In fact, the patient is the same in both sentences, and sentence (2) is an example of implicit middle voice. This has also been termed an anticausative.

COMPARING TRANSITIVE AND INTRANSITIVE VERBS

Depending on the type of object they take, verbs may be transitive, intransitive, or linking.

The meaning of a transitive verb is incomplete without a direct object, as in the following examples:

INCOMPLETE

The shelf holds.

COMPLETE

The shelf holds three books and a vase of flowers.

INCOMPLETE

The committee named.

COMPLETE

The committee named a new chairperson.

INCOMPLETE

The child broke.

COMPLETE

The child broke the plate.

An intransitive verb, on the other hand, cannot take a direct object:

This plant has thrived on the south windowsill.

The compound verb "has thrived" is intransitive and takes no direct object in this sentence. The prepositional phrase "on the south windowsill" acts as an adverb describing where the plant thrives.

The sound of the choir carried through the cathedral.

The verb "carried" is used intransitively in this sentence and takes no direct object. The prepositional phrase "through the cathedral" acts as an adverb describing where the sound carried.

The train from Montreal arrived four hours late.

The intransitive verb "arrived" takes no direct object, and the noun phrase "four hours late" acts as an adverb describing when the train arrived.

Since the company was pleasant and the coffee both plentiful and good, we lingered in the restaurant for several hours.

The verb "lingered" is used intransitively and takes no direct object. The prepositional phrase "in the restaurant for several hours" acts as an adverb modifying "lingered".

The painting was hung on the south wall of the reception room.

The compound verb "was hung" is used intransitively and the sentence has no direct object. The prepositional phrase "on the south wall of the reception room" acts as a adverb describing where the paint hung.

Many verbs can be either transitive or intransitive, depending on their context in the sentence. In the following pairs of sentences, the first sentence uses the verb transitively and the second uses the same verb intransitively:

transitive

According to the instructions, we must *leave* this goo in our hair for twenty minutes.

In this example, the verb "leave" takes a direct object, the noun phrase "this goo".

intransitive

We would like to stay longer, but we must *leave*.

In this example, the verb "leave" does not take a direct object.

transitive

The audience attentively *watched* the latest production of The Trojan Women.

In this example, the verb "watch" is used transitively and takes the noun phrase "the latest production of The Trojan Women" as a direct object.

intransitive

The cook watched while the new dishwasher surreptitiously picked up the fragments of the broken dish.

In this example, the verb "watched" is used intransitively and takes no direct object.

intransitive

The crowd moves across the field in an attempt to see the rock star get into her helicopter.

Here the verb "moves" is used as an intransitive verb and takes no direct object.

transitive

Every spring, William moves all boxes and trunks from one side of the attic to the other.

In this sentence "moves" is used as a transitive verb and takes the noun phrase "all the boxes and trunk" as a direct object.

8

Active and Passive Voice

In grammar, the voice (also called gender or diathesis) of a verb describes the relationship between the action (or state) that the verb expresses and the participants identified by its arguments (subject, object, etc.). When the subject is the agent or actor of the verb, the verb is in the active voice. When the subject is the patient, target or undergoer of the action, it is said to be in the passive voice. For example, in the sentence:

— The cat ate the mouse

The verb "ate" is in the active voice, but in the sentence:

— The mouse was eaten by the cat

— the verbal phrase "was eaten" is passive.

In a transformation from an active-voice clause to an equivalent passive-voice construction, the subject and the direct object switch grammatical roles. The direct object gets promoted to subject, and the subject demoted to an (optional) complement. In the examples above, the mouse serves as the direct object in the active-voice version, but becomes the subject in the passive version. The subject of the active-voice version, the cat, becomes part of a prepositional phrase in the passive version of the sentence, and could be left out entirely.

Active voice is distinguished from passive voice by the identity of the actor. As a general rule, active voice is preferred because it meets two of the most important requirements of legal writing: clarity and conciseness. Active voice is clearer because it focuses the reader's attention on the "doer of the action"; it is also more concise simply because it usually involves fewer words.

While any single use of the passive voice is not technically incorrect, the repeated use of passive voice produces a sluggish, ponderous text. However, there are a limited number of situations -- explained below -- where using passive voice is preferable. The good writer will actively seek to avoid the passive voice unless presented with a strong justification for its use.

1. As a general rule, use active subject-verb formulations.

   Undesirable: A mistake was made by the lawyer, and a mistrial was declared by the judge.

   Better: The lawyer made a mistake, and the judge declared a mistrial.

   Undesirable: The heinous murders were committed by the defendant.

   Better: The defendant committed the heinous murders.

2. Use passive voice when intentionally trying to hide the identity of the actor. In the following

example, the writer (defense counsel) prefers not to use the active voice in order to avoid focusing attention on the identity of the actor.

Acceptable: The body was removed from the crime scene.

3. Use passive voice if it produces greater emphasis on the main point of the sentence.

   If use of the active voice diminishes the point of the sentence, one may use passive voice instead. In the following example, the writer achieves a greater emphasis on poor people -- rather than the legislature -- by using the passive voice.

   Undesirable: The legislature should not crucify the poor on the cross of a balanced budget.

   Better: The poor should not be crucified on the cross of a balanced budget.

4. You may use passive voice with a multi-part subject. If the subject of the sentence is so long or complex that the reader will be long delayed in reaching the verb, then the writer may choose to place the verb before the subject. Either of the approaches below may be acceptable for a given audience.

   Acceptable Active Formulation: The committee reports, the floor debates, the presidential statement, and the administrative agency's interpretive guidance mandate the statutory interpretation we have chosen.

   Acceptable Passive Formulation: The statutory interpretation we have chosen is mandated by the committee reports, the floor debates, the presidential statement, and the administrative agency's interpretive guidance.

For active voice sentences, the verb is the action element of the sentence, the subject is the "doer" of the action, and the object is the recipient of the action. Active sentences have their three elements in this order: subject, verb, object. This is not true for sentences constructed in the passive voice. The subject is not "doer" of the action; the object becomes the "doer" of the action. These sentences flip-flop the subject and the object. For example, consider the following sentences:

Active voice:

— Laura invited Nancy to a party this Saturday night at 8:00.

— Robins eat huge amounts of earth worms every spring.

— Farmers predominantly raise corn and hogs in Iowa.

— Scholars have translated that book into sixteen different languages.

Passive voice:

— Nancy was invited to a party this Saturday night at 8:00.

— Huge amounts of earth worms are eaten every spring by robins.

— Predominantly, corn and hogs are raised in Iowa.

— This book has been translated into sixteen different languages.

Many times we are given the advice to avoid the passive voice. Usually, good writing uses the active voice and shuns the passive. However, sometimes the active voice is awkward or inappropriate. We use the passive voice frequently in speaking and writing—quite appropriately.

The first sentence, above, about the party, is a good example of this. The active voice sentence focuses on Laura, the person who did the inviting. The passive voice sentence focuses on Nancy, a potential party attendee. Deciding which sentence is best depends on your focus—what you wish to stress. When considering the last example sentence (the one about the book translation), the passive voice version actually sounds much better because we wish to focus on the book (which received the action of translation) not on the agent or person who performed the action.

As a general rule, however, the active voice is shorter, more direct, and more dynamic than the passive voice. When you are writing, try to find all of your passive sentences and change them into the active voice. Keep those sentences for which this is an improvement and return to your first construction for the others.

Examples of Active Voice

Ttransitive verbs are the only kind that can express action so as to go over to an object. This implies three things: the agent or person or thing acting; the verb representing the action; and the person or object receiving the act

We reached the village by dusk, and accepted the invitation of an old dame to lodge at her inn.

The three things found are: the actor or agent expressed by *we;* the action is asserted by *reached* and *accepted;* the things acted upon are *village* and *invitation.* Here, the subject is represented as doing something. The some word is the subject and the agent. This use of a transitive verb is called the active voice.

The active voice is that form of a verb which represents the subject as acting. It is that form of a transitive verb which makes the subject and the agent the same word. A verb is in the active voice when its form shows that the person or thing denoted by the subject is the doer of the action.

Examples:

1. He invited me to visit him.
2. Agatha Christie wrote many books.
3. My sister baked me a cake.
4. He studied the report carefully.
5. *He struck the man dead.*

Active voice can be changed into passive voice.

Examples:

1. Active : My father will write a letter.

   A letter will be written by my father.
2. Active: The hunter shot the lion.

   Passive: The lion was shot by the hunter.
3. Active: He threw the ball.

   Passive: The ball was thrown by him.

4. Active: He scored twenty runs.

   Passive: Twenty runs were scored by him.

5. Active: The police arrested him.

   Passive: He was arrested by the police.

Passive voice can be changed into active voice.

1. Passive: I was struck by his singular appearance.

   Active: His singular appearance struck me.

2. Passive: The town was destroyed by an earthquake.

   Active: An earthquake destroyed the town.

3. Passive: French fleet was defeated by Nelson.

   Active: Nelson defeated the French fleet.

4. Passive: The streets were thronged with spectators.

   Active: Spectators thronged the streets.

5. Passive: He was taken to the hospital by his friends.

   Active: His friends took him to the hospital.

It will be noticed that in the active voice, the objective of the transitive verb becomes the subject of the verb in the passive voice. In example 2 of Active to Passive transformation, the object *lion* in the active voice becomes the subject in the passive voice. It therefore follows that only transitive verbs can be used in the passive voice, because an intransitive verb has no object. It is important to know when to use the active voice and when to use the passive voice. When the subject is more important than the object, then active voice is used. The passive is used when the person or thing acted upon is to be made prominent. Generally, the passive voice is preferred when the active form involves the use of un indefinite or vague pronoun or noun, like, *they, somebody, people, we,* etc.

PASSICE VOICE

In English, as in many other languages, the passive voice is the form of a transitive verb whose grammatical subject serves as the patient, receiving the action of the verb. The passive voice is typically contrasted with the active voice, which is the form of a transitive verb whose subject serves as the agent, performing the action of the verb. The subject of a verb in the passive voice corresponds to the object of the same verb in the active voice. English's passive voice is periphrastic; that is, it does not have a one-word form. Rather, it is formed using a form of the auxiliary verb be together with a verb's past participle. Passive voice can be used in any number of tenses.

Canonical Passives

Passive constructions have a range of meanings and uses. The canonical use is to map a clause with a direct object to a corresponding clause where the direct object has become the subject. For example:

— John threw the ball.

Here threw is a transitive verb with John as its subject and the ball as its direct object. If we recast the verb in the passive voice (was thrown), then the ball becomes the subject (it is promoted to the subject position) and John disappears:

— The ball was thrown.

The original subject can typically be re-inserted using the preposition by:

— The ball was thrown by John.

Promotion of other Objects

One non-canonical use of English's passive is to promote an object other than a direct object. It is usually possible in English to promote indirect objects as well. For example:

— John gave Mary a book →Mary was given a book.

— John gave Mary a book. →Mary was given a book by John.

In the active form, gave is the verb; John is its subject, Mary its indirect object, and a book its direct object. In the passive forms, the indirect object has been promoted and the direct object has been left in place. It is also possible, in some cases, to promote the object of a preposition:

— They talked about the problem.→The problem was talked about.

In the passive form here, the preposition is "stranded"; that is, it is not followed by an object. Indeed, in some sense it doesn't have an object, since "the problem" is actually the subject of the sentence.

Promotion of Content Clauses

It is possible to promote a content clause that serves as a direct object. In this case, however, it typically does not change its position in the sentence, and an expletive it takes the normal subject position:

— They say that he left. It is said that he left.

Stative Passives

The passives described so far have all been eventive (or dynamic) passives. There exist also stative (or static, or resultative) passives; rather than describing an action, they describe the result of an action. English does not usually distinguish between the two. For example:

— The rule was broken.

This sentence has two different meanings, roughly the following:

— [Someone] broke (violated) the rule.

— The rule was in the broken (dysfunctional) state.

The former meaning represents the canonical, eventive passive; the latter, the stative passive. (The terms eventive and stative/resultative refer to the tendencies of these forms to describe events and resultant states, respectively. The terms can be misleading, however, as the canonical passive of a stative verb is not a stative passive, even though it describes a state.)

Some verbs do not form stative passives. In some cases, this is because distinct adjectives exist for this purpose, such as with the verb open:

— The door was opened. → [Someone] opened the door.

— The door was open. → The door was in the open state.

Adjectival passives

Adjectival passives are not true passives; they occur when a participial adjective (an adjective derived from a participle) is used predicatively. For example:

— She was relieved to find her car undamaged.

Here, relieved is an ordinary adjective, though it derives from the past participle of relieve.

In some cases, the line between an adjectival passive and a stative passive may be unclear.

Passives without Active Counterparts

In a few cases, passive constructions retain all the sense of the passive voice, but do not have immediate active counterparts. For example:

— He was rumored to be a war veteran. → [Someone] rumored him to be a war veteran.

(The asterisk here denotes an ungrammatical construction.) Similarly:

— It was rumored that he was a war veteran. → *[Someone] rumored that he was a war veteran.

In both of these examples, the active counterpart was once possible, but has fallen out of use.

Double Passives

It is possible for a verb in the passive voice - especially an object-raising verb - to take an infinitive complement that is also in the passive voice:

— The project is expected to be completed in the next year.

Commonly, either or both verbs may be moved into the active voice:

- [Someone] expects the project to be completed in the next year.
- [Someone] is expected to complete the project in the next year.
- [Someone] expects [someone] to complete the project in the next year.

In some cases, a similar construction may occur with a verb that is not object-raising in the active voice:

- The project will be attempted to be completed in the next year. *[Someone] will attempt the project to be completed in the next year. [Someone] will attempt to complete the project in the next year.

In this example, the object of the infinitive has been promoted to the subject of the main verb, and both the infinitive and the main verb have been moved to the passive voice.

Other passive Constructions

Past participle alone

A past participle alone usually carries passive force; the form of be can therefore be omitted in certain circumstances, such as signs, newspaper headlines, and reduced relative clauses:

- Couple found slain; Murder-suicide suspected.
- The problem, unless dealt with, will only get worse.

- A person struck by lightning has a high chance of survival.

With get as the auxiliary

While the ordinary passive construction uses the auxiliary be, using get in its place can sometimes achieve the same effect:

- Jamie got hit with the ball.

This use of get is fairly restricted. First of all, it is fairly colloquial; be is used in news reports, formal writing, and so on. Second, it typically only forms eventive passives of eventive verbs.

Ergative verbs

An ergative verb is a verb that may be either transitive or intransitive, and whose subject when it is intransitive plays the same semantic role as its direct object when it is transitive. For example, fly is an ergative verb, such that the following sentences are roughly synonymous:

- The airplane flew.
- The airplane was flown.
- [Someone] flew the airplane.

One major difference is that the intransitive construction does not permit an agent to be mentioned, and indeed can imply that no agent is present, that the subject is performing the action on itself. For this reason, the intransitive construction of an ergative verb is often said to be in a middle voice, between active and passive, or in a mediopassive voice, between active and passive but closer to passive.

Reflexive Verbs

A reflexive verb is a transitive verb one of whose objects is a reflexive pronoun (myself, yourself, etc.) referring back to its subject. In some languages, reflexive verbs are a special class of verbs with special semantics and syntax, but in English, they typically represent ordinary uses of transitive verbs. For example, with the verb see:

— He sees her as a writer.

— She sees herself as a writer.

Nonetheless, sometimes English reflexive verbs have a passive sense, expressing an agentless action. Consider the verb solve, as in the following sentences:

— He solved the problem.

— The problem solved itself.

One could not say that the problem truly solved anything; rather, what is meant is that the problem was solved without anyone's solving it.

Gerunds and Nominalization

Gerunds and nominalized verbs (nouns derived from verbs and referring to the actions or states expressed by them), unlike finite verbs, do not require explicit subjects. This allows an object to be expressed while omitting a subject. For example:

— The proof of the pudding is in the eating.

— Generating electricity typically requires a magnet and a solenoid.

The same applies to infinitive constructions:

— The easiest way to make more space would be to install more shelving.
— The first step is to read the manual.

Forming the Passive

The passive voice can be recognized through the use of a "double verb" and is formed by using a form of the verb "to be" and the past participle of another verb. The past participle of regular verbs is -ed added to the base form (such as mailed, walked, performed, stopped, surprised, etc.). Irregular verbs have different forms of the past participle (such as taught, bitten, rung, shut, etc.).

This is an example of the verb "stop" in the various forms of the passive:

— is stopped
— was stopped
— is being stopped
— has been stopped
— was being stopped
— had been stopped
— is going to be stopped
— will be stopped
— can be stopped
— should be stopped
— ought to be stopped
— must be stopped
— has to be stopped
— may be stopped

— might be stopped
— used to be stopped

Here is the verb "stop" in the various forms of the active:

— stops
— stopped
— is stopping
— has stopped
— was stopping
— had stopped
— is going to stop
— will stop
— can stop
— should stop
— ought to stop
— must stop
— has to stop
— may stop
— might stop
— used to stop

Here are the different forms of the verb "to be": be, am, is, are, was, were, been, being.

Sometimes, although the main focus is on the recipient of the action, it is also important to mention the "doer" of the action. In this case, we use a by phrase to indicate who or what performed the action:

- The earth worms are eaten by robins.
- The contract was signed by everyone.
- The bells are being rung every hour by our staff members.

Not all verbs can be used to form the passive voice. Only transitive verbs (verbs that are followed by an object) can form the passive.

Here are some common intransitive verbs: agree, arrive, come, cry, depart, exist, fall, go, happen, live, occur, rain, rise, sleep, stay, take place, stand, walk. These verbs will not form the passive voice.

The passive can occur in different verb tenses:

Active	Passive
My teacher helps me.	I am helped by my teacher.
My teacher helped me.	I was helped by my teacher.
My teacher will help me.	My teacher is going to help me.
I will be helped by my teacher.	I am going to be helped by my teacher.
My teacher has helped me.	I have been helped by my teacher.
My teacher had helped me.	I had been helped by my teacher.
My teacher will have helped me tomorrow.	I will have been helped by my teacher tomorrow.
My teacher is helping me.	I am being helped by my teacher.
My teacher was helping me.	I was being helped by my teacher.

Examples of Passive Voice

1. He was killed by his brother.
2. The exhibition was opened by Nobel Laureate Mother Teresa.

3. He is loved by all.
4. This letter was posted last night.
5. We are taught music by Mr. Victor.
6. The statue is being visited by hundreds of tourists every year.
7. My books were stolen by someone yesterday.
8. These books had been left in the classroom by a careless student.
9. Coffee is raised in many parts of Hawaii by plantation workers..
10. Their home had been broken into by someone while they were on vacation .

9

Linking Verbs

Linking verbs or copular verbs link a subject to a complement. Linking verbs must be followed by a complement in order to make the sentence complete. The complement can be a subject complement or an adverbial, and occurs in two sentence types which are of the Subject-Verb-Complement (SVC) and Subject-Verb-Adverbial (SVA) pattern.

Linking verb does not have much meaning in itself. It "links" the subject to what is said about the subject. Usually, a linking verb shows equality (=) or a change to a different state or place (>). Linking verbs are always intransitive (but not all intransitive verbs are linking verbs).

— Mary is a teacher. (mary = teacher)

— Tara is beautiful. (tara = beautiful)

— That sounds interesting. (that = interesting)

— The sky became dark. (the sky > dark)

— The bread has gone bad. (bread > bad)

TYPES

There are two groups of linking verbs: current linking verbs and resulting linking verbs.

Current linking verbs indicate a state. (current linking verbs) Resulting linking verbs indicate that the role of the verb complement is a result of the process described in the verb. (resulting linking verbs)

SENTENCE PATTERNS

Subject-Verb-Complement

We can distinguish the following patterns:

a. The complement is a noun phrase or noun clause:

   – This is a really nice outfit.

   – The anwer is that we don't want to go to the party.

   – He became a beggar.

b. To be can occur between the linking verb and the complement. Although this "to be" is not necessary, both American English and British English prefer an infinitive construction with to be rather than simply a noun phrase.

   – She seems (to be) all right.

   – He proved (to be) a good husband.

   – She appears (to be) exhausted.

Some linking verbs are restricted as to the words that may occur in their complement. Examples are: rest (assured), run (wild), plead (innocent), fall (silent).

Subject-Verb-Adverbial

The main linking verb that allows an adverbial as

complementation is to be. The most common adverbials are place and time adverbials.

- Tom is in the bathroom..
- My uncle lives in Belgium.
- The party will be at three o'clock.

The Verb BE:

Some grammarians refer to the verb be as "the copula" since this is its main function in English. All the forms of be can be used as a linking verb. Be is the main verb of the sentence, rather than the auxiliary and is used in both SVC and SVA patterns.

- I am at the office between 9 and 5.
- This is a really good class.
- Those books were very expensive.
- The students have been exhausted since the midterm.
- Their wedding will be in early May.

EXAMPLES

Linking verbs do not express action. Instead, they connect the subject of the verb to additional information about the subject. Look at the examples below:

- Keila is a shopaholic.
- Ising isn't something that Keila can do. Is connects the subject, Keila, to additional information about her, that she will soon have a huge credit card bill to pay.
- During the afternoon, my cats are content to nap on the couch.

— Areing isn't something that cats can do. Are is connecting the subject, cats, to something said about them, that they enjoy sleeping on the furniture.

— After drinking the old milk, Bladimiro turned green.

— Turned connects the subject, Bladimiro, to something said about him, that he was needing Pepto Bismol.

— A ten-item quiz seems impossibly long after a night of no studying.

— Seems connects the subject, a ten-item quiz, with something said about it, that its difficulty depends on preparation, not length.

— Irene always feels sleepy after pigging out on pizza from Antonio's.

— Feels connects the subject, Irene, to her state of being, sleepiness.

The following verbs are *true* linking verbs: any form of the verb be [am, is, are, was, were, has been, are being, might have been, etc.], become, and seem. These true linking verbs are *always* linking verbs.

Then you have a list of verbs with multiple personalities: appear, feel, grow, look, prove, remain, smell, sound, taste, and turn. Sometimes these verbs are linking verbs; sometimes they are action verbs.

How do you tell when they are action verbs and when they are linking verbs?

If you can substitute am, is, or are and the sentence still sounds logical, you have a *linking* verb on your hands.

If, after the substitution, the sentence makes no sense, you are dealing with an *action* verb instead. Here are some examples:

– Sylvia tasted the spicy squid eyeball stew.

– Sylvia is the stew? I don't think so! Tasted, therefore, is an action verb in this sentence, something Sylvia is *doing*.

– The squid eyeball stew tasted good.

– The stew is good? You bet. Make your own!

– I smell the delicious aroma of a mushroom and papaya pizza baking in the oven.

– I am the aroma? No way! Smell, in this sentence, is an action verb, something I am *doing*.

– The mushroom and papaya pizza smells heavenly.

– The pizza is heavenly? Definitely! Try a slice!

– When my dog Oreo felt the wet grass beneath her paws, she bolted up the stairs and curled up on the couch.

– Oreo is the wet grass? Of course not! Here, then, felt is an action verb, something Oreo is *doing*.

– My dog Oreo feels depressed after seven straight days of rain.

– Oreo is depressed? Without a doubt! Oreo hates the wet.

– This substitution will not work for appear. With appear, you have to analyze the function of the verb.

– Swooping out of the clear blue sky, the blue jay appeared on the branch.

— *Appear* is something a blue jay can *do*—especially when food is near.

— The blue jay appeared happy to see the bird feeder.

— Here, *appeared* is connecting the subject, the blue jay, to its state of mind, happiness.

10

Verbals

A verbal is a noun or adjective formed from a verb. Writers sometimes make mistakes by using a verbal in place of a verb, and in very formal writing, by confusing different types of verbals. This section covers three different verbals: the participle (which acts as an adjective), the gerund (which acts as a noun), and the infinitive (which also acts as a noun). The fundamental difference between verbals and other nouns and adjectives is that verbals can take their own objects, even though they are no longer verbs.

GERUNDS

A gerund is a verbal that ends in -ing and functions as a noun. The term verbal indicates that a gerund, like the other two kinds of verbals, is based on a verb and therefore expresses action or a state of being. However, since a gerund functions as a noun, it occupies some positions in a sentence that a noun ordinarily would, for example: subject, direct object, subject complement, and object of preposition.

Gerund as Subject:

- Traveling might satisfy your desire for new experiences. (Traveling is the gerund.)
- The study abroad program might satisfy your desire for new experiences. (The gerund has been removed.)

Gerund as Direct Object:.

- They do not appreciate my singing. (The gerund is singing.)
- They do not appreciate my assistance. (The gerund has been removed)

Gerund as Subject Complement:

- My cat's favorite activity is sleeping. (The gerund is sleeping.)
- My cat's favorite food is salmon. (The gerund has been removed.)

Gerund as Object of Preposition:

- The police arrested him for speeding. (The gerund is speeding.)
- The police arrested him for criminal activity. (The gerund has been removed.)

A Gerund Phrase is a group of words consisting of a gerund and the modifier(s) and/or (pro)noun(s) or noun phrase(s) that function as the direct object(s), indirect object(s), or complement(s) of the action or state expressed in the gerund, such as:

The gerund phrase functions as the subject of the sentence.

Finding a needle in a haystack would be easier than what we're trying to do.

Finding (gerund)

a needle (direct object of action expressed in gerund)

in a haystack (prepositional phrase as adverb)

The gerund phrase functions as the direct object of the verb appreciate.

I hope that you appreciate my offering you this opportunity.

my (possessive pronoun adjective form, modifying the gerund)

offering (gerund)

you (indirect object of action expressed in gerund)

this opportunity (direct object of action expressed in gerund)

The gerund phrase functions as the subject complement.

Newt's favorite tactic has been lying to his constituents.

lying to (gerund)

his constituents (direct object of action expressed in gerund)

The gerund phrase functions as the object of the preposition for.

You might get in trouble for faking an illness to avoid work.

faking (gerund)

an illness (direct object of action expressed in gerund)

to avoid work (infinitive phrase as adverb)

The gerund phrase functions as the subject of the sentence.

Being the boss made Jeff feel uneasy.

Being (gerund)

the boss (subject complement for Jeff, via state of being expressed in gerund)

Punctuation

A gerund virtually never requires any punctuation with it. Points to remember:

1. A gerund is a verbal ending in -ing that is used as a noun.
2. A gerund phrase consists of a gerund plus modifier(s), object(s), and/or complement(s).
3. Gerunds and gerund phrases virtually never require punctuation.

Gerund and Infinitive

Although a gerund and an infinitive will often have practically the same meaning, there can be a difference in meaning.

Examples

a. Running in the park after dark can be dangerous. (gerund).

b. To run in the park after dark can be dangerous. (infinitive)

Gerunds are used to describe an "actual, vivid or fulfilled action", whereas infinitives are better used to describe "potential, hypothetical or future events". Although they are not, strictly speaking, verbs, gerunds and infinitives carry within them the idea of action. Combined with auxiliary verb forms, like verbs, they also express various shades of time.

Simple Forms

1. We planned to watch all the events of the Olympics.
2. Seeing those athletes perform is always a great thrill.

Perfect Forms

Examples

1. The women's team hoped to have won a gold medal before they were done.
2. We were thrilled about their having been in contention in the world championships before.

Passive Forms

Examples

1. To be chosen as an Olympian must be the biggest thrill in any athlete's life.
2. Being chosen, however, is probably not enough.

Perfect Passive Forms

Examples

1. The women did not seem satisfied simply to have been selected as players.
2. Having been honoured this way, they went out and earned it by winning the gold.

Perfect Continuous Infinitive

Example

To have been competing at that level, at our age already, was quite an accomplishment.

Gerund Phrases

A gerund phrase is a group of words consisting of a gerund and the modifier(s) and/or pronoun(s) or noun phrase(s) that function as the direct object(s), indirect object(s) or complement(s) of the action or state expressed in the gerund.

Examples

1. Finding a needle in a haystack would be easier than what we are trying to do.

   The gerund phrase functions as the subject of the sentence.

   Finding: gerund

   In a haystack: preposition phrase as adverb

   a needle: direct object of action expressed in gerund

2. I hope that you appreciate *my offering you this opportunity*.

   The gerund phrase functions as the direct object of the verb (*appreciate*).

   my: possessive pronoun objective form, modifying the gerund

   offering : gerund

   you: indirect object of action expressed in gerund

3. His favourite tactic has been lying to his constituents.

   The gerund phrase functions as the subject complement.

   lying to: gerund

   his constituents: direct object of action expressed in gerund.

4. you might get in trouble for faking an illness to avoid work.

   The gerund phrase functions as the object of the preposition *for*.

   faking: gerund

   to avoid work: infinitive phrase as adverb

5. *Being the boss made him fell uneasy.*

   The gerund phrase functions as the subject of the sentence.

   being: gerund

   the loss: subject complement for him, via state of being expressed in gerund.

   A gerund virtually never requires any punctuation with it.

In many compound nouns you will find gerunds.

Examples

1. walking-stick (a stick for walking)
2. frying-pan (a pan for frying)
3. fencing-stick (a stick for fencing)
4. writing-table (a table for writing
5. rolling-pin (a pin for rolling)

PARTICIPLES

A participle is a verbal that is used as an adjective and most often ends in -ing or -ed. The term verbal indicates that a participle, like the other two kinds of verbals, is based on a verb and therefore expresses action or a state of being. However, since they function as adjectives, participles modify nouns or pronouns. There are two types of participles: present participles and past participles. Present participles end in -ing. Past participles end in -ed, -en, -d, -t, or -n, as in the words asked, eaten, saved, dealt, and seen.

— The crying baby had a wet diaper.

— Shaken, he walked away from the wrecked car.

— The burning log fell off the fire.

— Smiling, she hugged the panting dog.

A participial phrase is a group of words consisting of a participle and the modifier(s) and/or (pro)noun(s) or noun phrase(s) that function as the direct object(s), indirect object(s), or complement(s) of the action or state expressed in the participle, such as:

Removing his coat, Jack rushed to the river.

The participial phrase functions as an adjective modifying Jack.

Removing (participle)

his coat (direct object of action expressed in participle)

Delores noticed her cousin walking along the shoreline.

The participial phrase functions as an adjective modifying cousin.

walking (participle)

along the shoreline (prepositional phrase as adverb)

Children introduced to music early develop strong intellectual skills.

The participial phrase functions as an adjective modifying children.

introduced (to) (participle)

music (direct object of action expressed in participle)

early (adverb)

Having been a gymnast, Lynn knew the importance of exercise.

The participial phrase functions as an adjective modifying Lynn.

Having been (participle)

a gymnast (subject complement for Lynn, via state of being expressed in participle)

Placement: In order to prevent confusion, a participial phrase must be placed as close to the noun it modifies as possible, and the noun must be clearly stated.

— Carrying a heavy pile of books, his foot caught on a step.

— Carrying a heavy pile of books, he caught his foot on a step.

In the first sentence there is no clear indication of who or what is performing the action expressed in the participle carrying. Certainly foot can't be logically understood to function in this way. This situation is an example of a dangling modifier error since the modifier (the participial phrase) is not modifying any specific noun in the sentence and is thus left "dangling." Since a person must be doing the carrying for the sentence to make sense, a noun or pronoun that refers to a person must be in the place immediately after the participial phrase, as in the second sentence.

Punctuation: When a participial phrase begins a sentence, a comma should be placed after the phrase.

— Arriving at the store, I found that it was closed.

— Washing and polishing the car, Frank developed sore muscles.

If the participle or participial phrase comes in the middle of a sentence, it should be set off with commas only if the information is not essential to the meaning of the sentence.

— Sid, watching an old movie, drifted in and out of sleep.

— The church, destroyed by a fire, was never rebuilt.

Note that if the participial phrase is essential to the meaning of the sentence, no commas should be used:

— The student earning the highest grade point average will receive a special award.

— The guy wearing the chicken costume is my cousin.

If a participial phrase comes at the end of a sentence, a comma usually precedes the phrase if it modifies an earlier word in the sentence but not if the phrase directly follows the word it modifies.

— The local residents often saw Ken wandering through the streets.

(The phrase modifies Ken, not residents.)

— Tom nervously watched the woman, alarmed by her silence.

(The phrase modifies Tom, not woman.)

Points to Remember

1. A participle is a verbal ending in -ing (present) or -ed, -en, -d, -t, or -n (past) that functions as an adjective, modifying a noun or pronoun.
2. A participial phrase consists of a participle plus modifier(s), object(s), and/or complement(s).
3. Participles and participial phrases must be placed as close to the nouns or pronouns they modify as possible, and those nouns or pronouns must be clearly stated.
4. A participial phrase is set off with commas when it:
   a) comes at the beginning of a sentence
   b) interrupts a sentence as a nonessential element
   c) comes at the end of a sentence and is separated from the word it modifies.

Present Participles

Present participles represent an action as going on or incomplete or imperfect. They end in -ing.

Examples

1. We saw a bird feeding its young.

2. Quality sitting by the river, she watched it flowing quietly.
3. The lion, licking its wounds, lay down on the grass.
4. Smiling, she bugged the brave dog.
5. The players returned, smiling broadly.

Past Participle

Past participles represent a completed action or state of the thing spoken of. They usually end in -ed, -d, -t or -n.

Examples

1. Shaken, he walked away from the wrecked car.
2. Chased by an angry dog, the man sped away.
3. We noticed the donkey laden with bags of cement.
4. Time misspent is time lost.
5. Beaten by the police, he confessed.

Perfect Participle

A perfect participle represents an action as completed at some past time.

Examples

1. Having finished his supper, he drank two glasses of water.
2. Having forgotten her friend's birthday, she sent flowers to her.
3. Not having been present, he missed the wonderful speech.

4. Having been rejected by the public, the film was withdrawn from theatres.
5. Having been identified as the culprit, the man confessed to his misdeeds.

Participial Phrase

A participial phrase is a group of words consisting of a participle and the modifiers(s) and/or pronoun(s) or noun(s) or noun phrase(s) that function as the direct object(s), indirect object(s), or complement(s) of the action or state expressed in the participle.

Examples

1. Removing his coat, Jack rushed to the river.

   The participial phrase removing his coat functions as an adjective modifying Jack. Removing is the participle.

2. She noticed her cousin walking along the shoreline.

   Walking along the shoreline, prepositional phrase modifying cousin.

   Walking: participle

   walking along the shoreline: participial phrase modifying cousin.

3. Children, introduced to music early, develop strong intellectual skills.

   introduced to music early: participial phrase modifying children.

   introduced to : participle

   music: direct object of action expressed in participle

early: adverb

4. Having been a gymnast, she knew the importance of exercise.

   Having been a gymnast: participial phrase modifying she.

   having been: participle

   a gymnast: subject complement for she.

In order to prevent confusion, a participial phrase must be placed as close as possible to the noun or pronoun it modifies, and the noun or pronoun must be clearly stated.

Examples

a. Carrying a heavy pile of books, he caught his foot on a step.

b. Carrying a heavy pile of books, he caught his foot on a step.

In the first sentence, there is no clear indication of who or what is performing the action expressed in the participle carrying. Certainly foot can't be logically understood to function in this way. This situation is an example of a dangling modifier error since the modifier (the participial phrase) is not modifying any specific noun in the sentence, and is thus left 'dangling'. Since a person must be doing the carrying for the sentence to make sense, a noun or pronoun that refers to a person must be in place immediately after the participial phrase, as in the second sentence.

a. Crossing the bridge, a courtyard lies in front of you.

b. A courtyard crosses the bridge and it lies in front of you.

In these sentences, clearly it was not the courtyard that crossed the bridge. The second sentence makes sense.

a. Wide-brimmed and furry, the prince raised his hat and waved it at the crowd.

b. (Correct sentence). The prince raised his hat, wide-brimmed and furry, and waved it at the crowd.

When a participial phrase begins a sentence, a comma should be placed after the phrase.

Examples

1. Arriving at the store, I found that it was closed.
2. Washing and polishing the car, Frank developed sore muscles.

If the participial phrase comes in the middle of a sentence, it should be set off with commas only if the information is not essential to the meaning of the sentence.

Examples

1. Sid, watching an old movie, drifted in and out of sleep.
2. The church, destroyed by a fire, was never rebuilt.

Note that if the participial phrase is essential to the meaning of the sentence, no commas should be used.

Examples

1. The student earning the highest grade point average will receive a special award.
2. The guy wearing the chiicken costume is my cousin.

If a participial phrase comes at the end of a sentence, a comma usually precedes the phrase if it modifies an earlier word in the sentence but not if the phrase directly follows the word it modifies.

Examples

1. The local residents often saw Anand wandering through the streets.

   The phrase wandering through the streets modifies Anand, not residents.

2. Anil nervously watched the woman, alarmed by her silence.

   The phrase alarmed by her silence modifies Anil not woman.

Use of the Participle

Continuous tenses (active voice) are formed from the present participle with tenses of the verb be.

Examples

1. I am loving. (present continuous)
2. I was loving. (past continuous
3. I shall be loving. (future continuous)

The perfect tenses (active voice) are formed from the past participle with tenses of the verb have.

Examples

1. I have loved. (present perfect)
2. I had loved. (past perfect)
3. I shall have loved. (future perfect)

The passive voice is formed from the past participle with tenses of the verb be.

Examples

1. I am loved. (present perfect)
2. I was loved. (past perfect)
3. I shall be loved. (future perfect)

Participles qualify nouns or pronouns, and may be used:

Attributively

Examples

1. A flying object landed here.
2. Her new pen writes well.

Predicatively

Examples

1. The girl looks harassed. (modifying the subject).
2. The book left me crying. (modifying the object)

Absolutely (with a noun or pronoun preceding)

Examples

1. The story being long, I shortened it.
2. The weather being pleasant, we set out.

INFINITIVES

An infinitive is a verbal consisting of the word to plus a verb (in its simplest "stem" form) and functioning as a noun, adjective, or adverb. The term verbal indicates that an infinitive, like the other two kinds of verbals, is based on a verb and therefore expresses action or a state of being. However, the infinitive may function as a subject, direct object, subject complement, adjective, or adverb in a sentence. Although an infinitive is easy to locate because of the to + verb form, deciding what function it has in a sentence can sometimes be confusing.

— To wait seemed foolish when decisive action was required. (subject)

— Everyone wanted to go. (direct object)

— His ambition is to fly. (subject complement)

— He lacked the strength to resist. (adjective)

— We must study to learn. (adverb)

Be sure not to confuse an infinitive-a verbal consisting of to plus a verb-with a prepositional phrase beginning with to, which consists of to plus a noun or pronoun and any modifiers.

— Infinitives: to fly, to draw, to become, to enter, to stand, to catch, to belong

— Prepositional Phrases: to him, to the committee, to my house, to the mountains, to us, to this address

An Infinitive Phrase is a group of words consisting of an infinitive and the modifier(s) and/or (pro)noun(s) or noun phrase(s) that function as the actor(s), direct object(s), indirect object(s), or complement(s) of the action or state expressed in the infinitive, such as:

We intended to leave early.

The infinitive phrase functions as the direct object of the verb intended.

to leave (infinitive)

early (adverb)

I have a paper to write before class.

The infinitive phrase functions as an adjective modifying paper.

to write (infinitive)

before class (prepositional phrase as adverb)

Phil agreed to give me a ride.

The infinitive phrase functions as the direct object of the verb agreed.

to give (infinitive)

me (indirect object of action expressed in infinitive)

a ride (direct object of action expressed in infinitive)

They asked me to bring some food.

The infinitive phrase functions as the direct object of the verb asked.

me (actor or "subject" of infinitive phrase)

to bring (infinitive)

some food (direct object of action expressed in infinitive)

Everyone wanted Carol to be the captain of the team.

The infinitive phrase functions as the direct object of the verb wanted.

Carol (actor or "subject" of infinitive phrase)

to be (infinitive)

the captain (subject complement for Carol, via state of being expressed in infinitive)

of the team (prepositional phrase as adjective)

Actors: In these last two examples the actor of the infinitive phrase could be roughly characterized as the "subject" of the action or state expressed in the infinitive. It is somewhat misleading to use the word subject, however, since an infinitive phrase is not a full clause with a subject and a finite verb. Also notice that when it is a pronoun, the actor appears in the objective case (me, not I, in the fourth example). Certain verbs, when they take an infinitive direct object, require an actor for the infinitive phrase; others can't have an actor. Still other verbs can go either way, as the charts below illustrate.

Verbs that take infinitive objects without actors:

agree	begin	continue	decide
fail	hesitate	hope	intend
learn	neglect	offer	plan
prefer	pretend	promise	refuse
remember	start	try	

Examples:

— Most students plan to study.

— We began to learn.

- They offered to pay.
- They neglected to pay.
- She promised to return.

In all of these examples no actor can come between the italicized main (finite) verb and the infinitive direct-object phrase.

Verbs that take infinitive objects with actors:

advise	allow	convince	remind
encourage	force	hire	teach
instruct	invite	permit	tell
implore	incite	appoint	order

Examples:

- He reminded me to buy milk.
- Their fathers advise them to study.
- She forced the defendant to admit the truth.
- You've convinced the director of the program to change her position.
- I invite you to consider the evidence.

In all of these examples an actor is required after the italicized main (finite) verb and before the infinitive direct-object phrase.

Verbs that use either pattern:

ask	expect	(would) like	want

Examples:

- I asked to see the records.
- I asked him to show me the records.

— Trent expected his group to win.

— Trent expected to win.

— Brenda likes to drive fast.

— Brenda likes her friend to drive fast.

In all of these examples the italicized main verb can take an infinitive object with or without an actor.

Punctuation: If the infinitive is used as an adverb and is the beginning phrase in a sentence, it should be set off with a comma; otherwise, no punctuation is needed for an infinitive phrase.

— To buy a basket of flowers, John had to spend his last dollar.

— To improve your writing, you must consider your purpose and audience.

Points to remember

1. An infinitive is a verbal consisting of the word to plus a verb; it may be used as a noun, adjective, or adverb.
2. An infinitive phrase consists of an infinitive plus modifier(s), object(s), complement(s), and/or actor(s).
3. An infinitive phrase requires a comma only if it is used as an adverb at the beginning of a sentence.

Split Infinitives

Split infinitives occur when additional words are included between to and the verb in an infinitive. Many readers find a single adverb splitting the infinitive to be acceptable, but this practice should be avoided in formal writing.

Examples:

— I like to on a nice day walk in the woods. (unacceptable)

  On a nice day, I like to walk in the woods. (revised)

— I needed to quickly gather my personal possessions. (acceptable in informal contexts)

  I needed to gather my personal possessions quickly. (revised for formal contexts)

Use of the Infinite

Although an infinitive is easy to locate because of the to + verb form, deciding what function it has in a sentence can sometimes be confusing.

An infinitive may function as a subject, direct object, subject complement, adjective, or adverb in a sentence.

Examples

1. To wait seemed foolish when decisive was required. (subject)
2. Everyone wanted to go. (direct object).
3. His ambition is to fly (subject complement).
4. He lacked the strength to resist. (adjective).
5. *We must study to learn. (adverb).*

Be sure not to confuse an infinitive a verb consisting of *to plus* verb—with a prepositional phrase beginning with *to* which consists of *to plus noun* (or pronoun or any modifier).

The infinitive, with or without adjuncts, may be used like a noun.

As the subject of a verb :

Examples

a. To err is human.

b. To criticise is easy.

As the object of a transitive verb:

Examples

a. I like to read novels

b. They like to play football.

As the complement of a verb:

Examples

a. His greatest ambition is to sing.

b. Her daily regimen is to dance daily.

As the object of a preposition

Examples

a. He had no alternative but to yield.

b. The ceremony is about to commence.

As an objective complement

1. I saw him read.
2. I saw him go.

When used like a noun, the infinitive is called the Simple Infinitive. The infinitive is used to qualify a verb, usually to express purpose.

Examples

1. We eat to live.

2. I work to earn.

The infinitive is used to qualify an adjective.

Examples

1. Apples are good to eat.
2. Children are eager to sing.

The infinitive is used to qualify a noun.

Examples

1. This is not the place to visit.
2. He is a man to be shunned.

The infinitive is used to qualify a sentence.

Examples

1. To tell you honestly I forget about the party.
2. He was shocked, to put it bluntly.

Infinitive Phrases

An infinitive phrase is a group of words consisting of an infinitive and the modifier(s) and/or pronoun(s) or noun(s) or noun phrase(s) that function as the doer, direct object, indirect object or complement of the action or state expressed in the infinitive.

Examples

1. *We intended to leave early.*

   The infinitive phrase functions as the direct object of the verb intended.

to leave: infinitive

early: adverb

2. *I have a paper to write before class.*

   The infinitive phrase functions as an adjective, modifying paper.

   to write: infinitive.

   before class: prepositional phrase as adverb

3. *Phil agreed to give me a ride.*

   The infinitive phrase functions as the direct object of the verb *agreed*.

   to give: infinitive

   me: indirect object of action expressed in infinitive

4. *They asked me to bring some food.*

   The infinitive phrase functions as the direct object of the verb *asked*.

   to bring: infinitive

   me: subject of the infinitive phrase.

   some food: direct object of action expressed in infinitive

5. *Everyone wanted Carol to be the captain of the team.*

   The infinitive phrase functions as the direct object of the verb *wanted*.

   carol: subject of the infinitive phrase to be: infinitive

   the captain: subject complement for Carol

   of the team: prepositional phrase as adjective.

Verbs Taking Infinitive Objects Without Actors

In the following examples you will observe that no actor can come between the underlined main verb and the infinitive direct object phrases.

Examples

1. Most students plan to study.
2. We began to learn.
3. They offered to pay
4. They neglected to pay.
5. She promised to return.

Verbs taking Infinitive objects with Actors

In all the following examples the underlined main verb can take an infinitive object with or without an actor.

1. He reminded me to buy milk.
2. She forced the defendant to admit the truth.
3. You have convinced the director to change her position.
4. I invite you to consider the evidence.
5. He advised her to study.

COMPARING GERUNDS AND PARTICIPLES

Look at the following pair of sentences. In the first, the use of a gerund (functioning as a noun) allows the meaning to be expressed more precisely than in the second. In the first sentence the interrupting itself, a specific behavior, is precisely indicated as the cause of the speaker's irritation. In the second the cause of the irritation is identified less precisely as Bill, who just happens to have been interrupting. (In the second sentence, interrupting is actually a participle, not a gerund, since it functions as an adjective modifying Bill.)

I was irritated by Bill's constant interrupting.

I was irritated by Bill, constantly interrupting.

The same pattern is shown in these other example pairs below: in the first of each pair, a gerund (noun-function) is used; in the second, a participle (adjective-function). Notice the subtle change in meaning between the two sentences in each pair.

Examples:

— The guitarist's finger-picking was extraordinary. (The technique was extraordinary.)

— The guitarist, finger-picking, was extraordinary. (The person was extraordinary, demonstrating the technique.)

— He was not impressed with their competing. (The competing did not impress him.)

— He was not impressed with them competing. (They did not impress him as they competed.)

— Grandpa enjoyed his grandchildren's running and laughing.

— Grandpa enjoyed his grandchildren, running and laughing.

COMPARING GERUNDS AND INFINITIVES

The difference in the form of gerunds and infinitives is quite clear just from comparing the following lists:

- Gerunds: swimming, hoping, telling, eating, dreaming
- Infinitives: to swim, to hope, to tell, to eat, to dream

Their functions, however, overlap. Gerunds always function as nouns, but infinitives often also serve as nouns. Deciding which to use can be confusing in many situations, especially for people whose first language is not English.

Confusion between gerunds and infinitives occurs primarily in cases in which one or the other functions as the direct object in a sentence. In English some verbs take gerunds as verbal direct objects exclusively while other verbs take only infinitives and still others can take either. Many such verbs are listed below, organized according to which kind of verbal direct object they take.

Verbs that take only infinitives as verbal direct objects:

agree	decide	expect	hesitate
learn	need	promise	neglect
hope	want	plan	attempt
propose	intend	pretend	

Examples:

- I hope to go on a vacation soon.

  (not: I hope going on a vacation soon.)
- He promised to go on a diet.

  (not: He promised going on a diet.)

— They agreed to sign the treaty.
(not: They agreed signing the treaty.)

— Because she was nervous, she hesitated to speak.
(not: Because she was nervous, she hesitated speaking.)

— They will attempt to resuscitate the victim
(not: They will attempt resuscitating the victim.)

Verbs that take only gerunds as verbal direct objects:

deny	risk	delay	consider
can't help	keep	give up	be fond of
finish	quit	put off	practice
postpone	tolerate	suggest	stop (quit)
regret	enjoy	keep (on)	dislike
admit	avoid	recall	mind
miss	detest	appreciate	recommend

Examples:

— They always avoid drinking before driving.
(not: They always avoid to drink before driving.)

— I recall asking her that question.
(not: I recall to ask her that question.)

— She put off buying a new jacket.
(not: She put off to buy a new jacket.)

— Mr. Allen enjoys cooking.
(not: Mr. Allen enjoys to cook.)

— Charles keeps calling her.
(not: Charles keeps to call her.)

Verbs that take gerunds or infinitives as verbal direct objects

start	begin	continue	hate
prefer	like	love	try
remember			

Examples:

— She has continued to work at the store.

She has continued working at the store.

— They like to go to the movies.

They like going to the movies.

— Brent started to walk home.

Brent started walking home.

Forget and Remember

These two verbs change meaning depending on whether a gerund or infinitive is used as the object.

Examples:

— Jack forgets to take out the cat. (He regularly forgets.)

Jack forgets taking out the cat. (He did it, but he doesn't remember now.)

— Jack forgot to take out the cat. (He never did it.)

Jack forgot taking out the cat. (He did it, but he didn't remember sometime later.)

— Jack remembers to take out the cat. (He regularly remembers.)

Jack remembers taking out the cat. (He did it, and he remembers now.)

— Jack remembered to take out the cat. (He did it.)
Jack remembered taking out the cat.

In the second of each pair of example sentences above, the past progressive gerund form having taken can be used in place of taking to avoid any possible confusion.

Sense verbs that take an object plus a gerund or a simple verb

Certain sense verbs take an object followed by either a gerund or a simple verb (infinitive form minus the word to). With many of the verbs that follow the object, the use of the gerund indicates continuous action while the use of the simple verb indicates a one-time action. Still, sometimes the simple verb can indicate continuous action if one-time action wouldn't make sense in the context.

feel	hear	notice	watch
see	smell	observe	

Examples:

— We watched him playing basketball. (continuous action)
We watched him play basketball. (continuous action)

— I felt my heart pumping vigorously. (continuous action)
I felt my heart pump vigorously. (continuous action)

— She saw them jumping on the bed. (continuous action)

- She saw them jump on the bed. (one-time action)
- Tom heard the victim shouting for help. (continuous action)

  Tom heard the victim shout for help. (one-time action)
- The detective noticed the suspect biting his nails. (continuous action)

  The detective noticed the suspect bite his nails. (one-time action)
- We could smell the pie baking in the kitchen. (continuous action)

  We could smell the pie bake in the kitchen. (continuous action)

Sometimes the simple-verb version might seem unconventional, so it's safer in most cases to use the gerund version.

11

Number and Person

NUMBER

Grammatical number is a grammatical category of nouns, pronouns, and adjective and verb agreement that expresses count distinctions (such as "one" or "more than one"). The count distinctions typically, but not always, correspond to the actual count of the referents of the marked noun or pronoun.

The word "number" is also used in linguistics to describe the distinction between certain grammatical aspects that indicate the number of times an event occurs, such as the semelfactive aspect, the iterative aspect, etc. For that use of the term, see "Grammatical aspect".

Most languages of the world have formal means to express differences of number. The most widespread distinction, as found in English and many other languages, involves a simple two-way number contrast between singular and plural (car / cars; child / children, etc.).

Grammatical number is a morphological category characterized by the expression of quantity through inflection or agreement.

As an example, consider the English sentences below:

— That apple on the table is fresh.

— Those two apples on the table are fresh.

The number of apples is marked on the noun - "apple", singular number (one item) vs. "apples", plural number (more than one item) -, on the demonstrative, "that/those", and on the verb, "is/are". Note that, especially in the second sentence, this information can be considered redundant, since quantity is already indicated by the numeral "two".

A language has grammatical number when its nouns are subdivided into morphological classes according to the quantity they express, such that:

1. Every noun belongs to a single number class. (Number partitions nouns into disjoint classes.)
2. Noun modifiers (such as adjectives) and verbs have different forms for each number class, and must be inflected to match the number of the nouns they refer to. (Number is an agreement category.)

This is the case in English: every noun is either singular or plural (a few, such as "fish", can be either, according to context), and at least some modifiers of nouns - namely the demonstratives, the personal pronouns, the articles, and verbs - are inflected to agree with the number of the nouns they refer to: "this car" and "these cars" are correct, while "this cars" or "these car" are ungrammatical.

Not all languages have number as a grammatical category. In those that do not, quantity must be expressed either directly, with numerals, or indirectly, through optional quantifiers. However, many of these languages compensate for the lack of grammatical number with an extensive system of measure words.

There is a hierarchy among number categories: No language distinguishes a trial unless having a dual, and no language has dual without a plural.

English is typical of most world languages, in distinguishing only between singular and plural number. The plural form of a word is usually created by adding the suffix -(e)s. Common exceptions include the pronouns, which have irregular plurals, as in I versus we, because they are ancient and frequently used words.

Regular Plurals

The plural morpheme in English is suffixed to the end of most nouns. The plural form is usually represented orthographically by adding -s to the singular form. The phonetic form of the plural morpheme is [z] by default. Examples:

boy boys

girl girls

chair chairs

When the preceding sound is a voiceless consonant-such as [t], [p], or [k]-it is pronounced [s]. Examples:

cat cats

lap laps

clock clocks

Where a noun ends in a sibilant sound-[s], [z] or the plural is formed by adding [z] which is spelled -es if the word does not already end with -e:

dish	dishes
glass	glasses
judge	judges
phase	phases
witch	witches

Morphophonetically, these rules are sufficient to describe most English plurals. However, there are several complications introduced in spelling.

The -oes rule: most nouns ending in o preceded by a consonant also form their plurals by adding -es (pronounced [z]):

hero	heroes
potato	potatoes
volcano	volcanoes or volcanos

The -ies rule: nouns ending in a y preceded by a consonant usually drop the y and add -ies (pronounced [iz]). This is taught to many American and British students with the rhyme: "Change the y to i and add es":

cherry	cherries
lady	ladies

However, proper nouns (particularly those for people or places) ending in a y preceded by a consonant form their plurals regularly:

Germany Germanys (as in The two Germanys were unified in 1990; this rule is

	commonly not adhered to as several book titles show, and Sicilies rather than Sicilys is the standard plural of Sicily)
Harry	Harrys (as in There are three Harrys in our office)

The rule does not apply to words that are merely capitalized common nouns:

P&O Ferries (from ferry)

Other exceptions include lay-bys and stand-bys.

Words ending in a y preceded by a vowel form their plurals regularly:

day	days
monkey	monkeys

(Money/Monies is an exception, but money can also form its plural regularly)

Almost-regular Plurals

Many nouns of foreign origin, including almost all Italian loanwords, are exceptions to the -oes rule:

canto	cantos
piano	pianos
portico	porticos
quarto (paper size)	quartos
kimono	kimonos

Many nouns ending in a voiceless fricative mutate those sounds to a voiced fricative before adding the plural ending. In the case of [f] changing to [v] the mutation is indicated in the orthography as well; also, a silent e is added in this case if the singular does not already end with -e:

bath	baths
house	houses
mouth	mouths
calf	calves
knife	knives

In practice, many people[who?] do not change the fricative, and instead use regular plurals.

Some retain the voiceless consonant:

moth	moths
place	places
proof	proofs

Some can do either:

dwarf	dwarfs/dwarves
hoof	hoofs/hooves
roof	roofs/rooves (latter archaic)
staff	staffs/staves
turf	turfs/turves (latter rare)

For dwarf, the common form of the plural was dwarfs-as, for example, in Walt Disney's Snow White and the Seven Dwarfs-until J. R. R. Tolkien popularized dwarves; he intended the changed spelling to differentiate the "dwarf" fantasy race in his novels from the cuter and simpler beings common in fairy tales, but his usage has since spread. Multiple astronomical dwarf stars and multiple nonmythological short human beings, however, remain dwarfs.

For staff in the sense of "a body of employees", the plural is always staffs; otherwise, both staffs and staves are acceptable, except in compounds; such as flagstaffs. Staves is rare in North America except in the sense of "magic rod." The stave of a barrel or cask is a back-formation from staves, which is its plural.

Irregular Plurals

There are many other less regular ways of forming plurals, usually stemming from older forms of English or from foreign borrowings.

Nouns with identical singular and plural

Some nouns spell their singular and plural exactly alike; some linguists regard these as regular plurals. Many of these are the names of animals:

- deer
- fish/fishes
- moose
- sheep
- swine

The plural deers is listed in some dictionaries, but is considered by many to be an error.

Fish does have a regular plural form, but it differs in meaning from the unmarked plural; fishes refers to several species or other taxonomic types, while fish (plural) is used to describe multiple individual animals: one would say "the order of fishes," but "five fish in an aquarium." The plural fishes is found in the King James Bible, in the miracle of the loaves and fishes, for example, and is sometimes used for rhetorical emphasis, as in phrases like sleep with the fishes.

Other nouns that have identical singular and plural forms include:

- aircraft
- blues
- cannon (sometimes cannons)
- head

Referring to individual songs in the blues musical style: "play me a blues"; "he sang three blues and a calypso"

Referring, in the plural, to animals in a herd: "fifty head of cattle"

Irregular -(e)n Plurals

The plural of a few nouns can also be formed from the singular by adding -n or -en, stemming from the obsolete Old English weak declension:

ox	oxen	(particularly when referring to a team of draft animals, sometimes oxes e.g. in a metaphorical sense)
cow	kine	(archaic/regional; actually earlier plural "kye" plus -en suffix, forming a double plural)
egg	eyren/eggys	(rare/dialectal Northern England & Scotland)

eye	eyen	(rare, found in some regional dialects)
shoe	shoon	(rare/dialectal)
house	housen	(rare/dialectal, used by Rudyard Kipling in Puck of Pook's Hill)
hose	hosen	(rare/archaic, used in King James Version of the Bible)
brother	brethren	(archaic plural of brother; earlier "brether" plus -en suffix, forming a double plural; now used in fraternal order)
child	children	(actually earlier plural "cildra/cildru" plus -en suffix, forming a double plural)

The word box, referring to a computer, is semi-humorously pluralized boxen in the Leet dialect. Multiple Vax computers, likewise, are sometimes called Vaxen particularly if operating as a cluster, but multiple Unix systems are usually Unices

Umlaut Plurals

The plural is sometimes formed by simply changing the vowel sound of the singular, in a process called umlaut (these are sometimes called mutated plurals):

foot	feet
goose	geese
louse	lice
man	men
mouse	mice

tooth	teeth
woman	women

Mouse is sometimes pluralized mouses in discussions of the computer mouse; however, mice is just as common.

Plurals of Numbers

English, like some other languages, treats large numerals as nouns (cf. "there were ten soldiers" and "there were a hundred soldiers"). Thus, dozens is preferred to tens, while hundreds and thousands are also completely acceptable.

Plurals of numbers differ according to how they are used. The following rules apply to dozen, score, hundred, thousand, million, and similar terms:

- When modified by a number, the plural is not inflected, that is, has no -s added. Hence one hundred, two hundred, etc. For vaguer large numbers, one may say several hundred or many hundreds.
- When used alone, or followed by a prepositional phrase, the plural is inflected: dozens of complaints, scores of people. However, either complaints by the dozen or complaints by the dozens is acceptable (although differing in meaning).
- The preposition of is used when speaking of nonspecific items identified by pronouns: two hundred of these, three dozen of those. The of is not used for a number of specific items: three hundred oriental rugs. However, if the pronoun

is included with the specific item, the of is used: five million of those dollar bills.

PERSON

Grammatical person, in linguistics, is deictic reference to a participant in an event, such as the speaker, the addressee, or others. Grammatical person typically defines a language's set of personal pronouns. It also frequently affects verbs, sometimes nouns, and possessive relationships as well.

English distinguishes three grammatical persons: The personal pronouns I (singular) and we (plural) are in the first person. The personal you is in the second person. It refers to the addressee. You is used in both the singular and plural; thou is the archaic informal second-person singular pronoun.

He, she, it, and they are in the third person. Any person, place, or thing other than the speaker and the addressee is referred to in the third person.

See English personal pronouns, and the following articles on specific grammatical persons, or their corresponding personal pronouns:

Pronoun	Person/plurality
I	First person singular
You	Second person singular/plural
He	Third person singular
She	Third person singular
It	Third person singular, neuter
We	First person plural
They	Third person plural

Colloquial	
You guys	Second person plural, colloquial US
You lot	Second person plural, colloquial UK
Y'all	Second person plural, dialect-
Youse	Second person plural, dialect-
Yinz	Second person plural, dialect-
Archiac	
Thou	Second person singular, archaic
Ye/you	Second person plural, archaic

Additional persons

In Indo-European languages, first-, second-, and third-person pronouns are all marked for singular and plural form, and sometimes dual form as well (see grammatical number). Some languages, especially European, distinguish degrees of formality and informality.

Other languages use different classifying systems, especially in the plural pronouns.One frequently found difference not present in most Indo-European languages is a contrast between inclusive and exclusive "we", a distinction of first-person pronouns of including or excluding the addressee.

Other languages have much more elaborate systems of formality that go well beyond the T-V distinction, and use many different pronouns and verb forms that express the speaker's relationship with the people he or she addresses. Many Malayo-Polynesian languages, such as Javanese and Balinese are well known for their complex systems of honorifics; Japanese and Korean also have similar systems to a lesser extent.

In many languages, the verb takes a form dependent on this person and whether it is singular or plural. In English, this happens with the verb to be as follows:

— I am (first-person singular)
— you are/thou art (second-person singular)
— he, she, one or it is (third-person singular)
— we are (first-person plural)
— you are (second-person plural)
— they are (third-person plural)

By contrast, Interlingua uses a single verb form for the three persons: es for is, am, and are, ha for has and have, and so on.

The grammars of some languages divide the semantic space into more than three persons. The extra categories may be termed fourth person, fifth person, etc. Such terms are not absolute but can refer depending on context to any of several phenomena.

Some languages, including among Algonquian languages and Salishan languages, divide the category of third person into two parts: proximate for a more topical third person, and obviative for a less topical third person. The obviative is sometimes called the fourth person.

The term fourth person is also sometimes used for the category of indefinite or generic referents, that work like one in English phrases such as "one should be prepared" or people in people say that..., when the grammar treats them differently from ordinary third-person forms. For example, the so-called "passive tense" in Finnish and related languages is actually not a tense, and has the same meaning as a phrase with subjects "one" or "people" in English.

12

Strong and Weak Verbs

Why do we say 'she jumped', 'he walked', 'they blinked', 'Homer nodded' but we don't say 'she thinked', 'he runned', 'they singed', and 'Homer speaked'? Or, to pose the question another way, why don't we say 'she jeamp', 'he wolk', 'they blank' or 'Homer nad'?

The answer is that English has two entirely separate systems of verbs: the 'weak' verbs, which form their past tenses by adding a dental suffix1 (usually the '-ed', although sometimes it is a '-t', or it is dropped altogether if the verb stem already ends with a dental sound); and the 'strong' verbs, which form their past tenses by a modification of the vowel sound in the root syllable of the verb.

The two types of verbs described here, strong and weak, do not comprise all verbs in the language. There is a different way of dividing the verbs into regular verbs, which comprises most of the weak verbs, and the irregular verbs, which describes the strong verbs, a number of weak verbs with irregular conjugations, and anomalous, or defective verbs. This entry is concerned only with the strong verbs and the weak verbs.

A strong verb forms its past tense by changing the vowel of the present tense form, but adds no ending; as, run, ran; drive, drove.

A weak verb always adds an ending to the present to form the past tense, and may or may not change the vowel: as, beg, begged; lay, laid; sleep, slept; catch, caught.

EXAMPLES OF STRONG VERBS

Some of examples of strong verb are given below:

Present tense	Past tense.	Past participle
abide	abode	abode
arise	arose	arisen
awake	awoke (awaked)	awoke (awaked)
bearbore	borne (active)	born (passive)
begin	began	begun
behold	beheld	beheld
bid	bade, bid	bidden, bid
bind	bound	bound,[adj. bounden]
bite	bit	bitten, bit
blow	blew	blown
break	broke	broken
chide	chid	chidden, chid
choose	chose	chosen
cleave	clove, clave (cleft)	cloven (cleft)
climb	[clomb] climbed	climbed

cling	clung	clung
come	came	come
crow	crew (crowed)	(crowed)
dig	dug	dug
do	did	done
draw	drew	drawn
drink	drank	drunk, drank, drunken
drive	drove	driven
eat	ate, eat	eaten, eat
fall	fell	fallen
fight	fought	fought
find	found	found
fling	flung	flung
fly	flew	flown
forbear	forbore	forborne
forget	forgot	forgotten
forsake	forsook	forsaken
freeze	froze	frozen
get	got	got [gotten]
give	gave	given
go	went	gone
grind	ground	ground
grow	grew	grown
hang	hung (hanged)	hung (hanged)

hold	held	held
know	knew	known
lie	lay	lain
ride	rode	ridden
ring	rang	rung
run	ran	run
see	saw	seen
shake	shook	shaken
shear	shore (sheared)	shorn (sheared)
shine	shone	shone
shoot	shot	shot
shrink	shrank or shrunk	shrunk
shrive	shrove	shriven
sing sang or	sung	sung
sink	sank or sunk	sunk [adj. sunken]
sit	sat [sate]	sat
slay	slew	slain
slide	slid	slidden, slid
sling	slung	slung
slink	slunk	slunk
smite	smote	smitten
speak	spoke	spoken
spin	spun	spun
spring	sprang, sprung	sprung
stand	stood	stood

stave	stove (staved)	(staved)
steal	stole	stolen
stick	stuck	stuck
sting	stung	stung
stink	stunk, stank	stunk
stride	strode	stridden
strike	struck	struck, stricken
string	strung	strung
strive	strove	striven
swear	swore	sworn
swim	swam or swum	swum
swing	swung	swung
take	took	taken
tear	tore	torn
thrive	throve (thrived)	thriven (thrived)
throw	threw	thrown
tread	trod	trodden, trod
wear	wore	worn
weave	wove	woven
win	won	won
wind	wound	wound
wring	wrung	wrung
write	wrote	written

REMARKS ON CERTAIN VERB FORMS.

Several of the perfect participles are seldom used except as adjectives: as, "his bounden duty," "the cloven hoof," "a drunken wretch," "a sunken snag." Stricken is used mostly of diseases; as, "stricken with paralysis."

The verb bear (to bring forth) is peculiar in having one participle (borne) for the active, and another (born) for the passive. When it means to carry or to endure, borne is also a passive.

The form clomb is not used in prose, but is much used in vulgar English, and sometimes occurs in poetry; as,-

- Thou hast clomb aloft.-Wordsworth
- Or pine grove whither woodman never clomb.-Coleridge

The forms of cleave are really a mixture of two verbs,-one meaning to adhere or cling; the other, to split. The former used to be cleave, cleaved, cleaved; and the latter, cleave, clave or clove, cloven. But the latter took on the weak form cleft in the past tense and past participle,-as (from Shakespeare), "O Hamlet! thou hast cleft my heart in twain,"-while cleave (to cling) sometimes has clove, as (from Holmes), "The old Latin tutor clove to Virgilius Maro." In this confusion of usage, only one set remains certain,-cleave, cleft, cleft (to split).

- Crew is seldom found in present-day English.
- Not a cock crew, nor a dog barked.-Irving.
- Our cock, which always crew at eleven, now told us it was time for repose.-Goldsmith.

Historically, drunk is the one correct past participle of the verb drink. But drunk is very much used as an adjective, instead of drunken (meaning intoxicated); and, probably to avoid confusion with this, drank is a good deal used as a past participle: thus,-

— We had each drank three times at the well.-B. Taylor.

— This liquor was generally drank by Wood and Billings. -Thackeray.

Sometimes in literary English, especially in that of an earlier period, it is found that the verb eat has the past tense and past participle eat (et), instead of ate and eaten; as, for example,-

— It ate the food it ne'er had eat.-Coleridge.

— How fairy Mab the junkets eat.-Milton.

— The island princes overbold

— Have eat our substance.

This is also very much used in spoken and vulgar English.

The form gotten is little used, got being the preferred form of past participle as well as past tense. One example out of many is,-

— We had all got safe on shore.-De Foe.

Hung and hanged both are used as the past tense and past participle of hang; but hanged is the preferred form when we speak of execution by hanging; as,

— The butler was hanged.-Bible.

The verb sat is sometimes spelled sate; for example,-

— Might we have sate and talked where gowans blow.-Wordsworth.

— He sate him down, and seized a pen.-Byron.

— "But I sate still and finished my plaiting."-Kingsley.

Usually shear is a weak verb. Shorn and shore are not commonly used: indeed, shore is rare, even in poetry.

— This heard Geraint, and grasping at his sword,
Shore thro' the swarthy neck.

Shorn is used sometimes as a participial adjective, as "a shorn lamb," but not much as a participle. We usually say, "The sheep were sheared" instead of "The sheep were shorn."

Went is borrowed as the past tense of go from the old verb wend, which is seldom used except in poetry; for example,-

If, maiden, thou would'st wend with me
To leave both tower and town.
-Scott.

WEAK VERBS

Those weak verbs which add -d or -ed to form the past tense and past participle, and have no change of vowel, are so easily recognized as to need no special treatment. Some of them are already given as secondary forms of the strong verbs.But the rest, which may be called irregular weak verbs, need some attention and explanation.

The irregular weak verbs are divided into two classes. The two classes of irregular weak verbs are:

(1) Those which retain the -d or -t in the past tense, with some change of form for the past tense and past participle.

(2) Those which end in -d or -t, and have lost the ending which formerly was added to this.

The old ending to verbs of Class II. was -de or -te; as,-

This worthi man ful wel his wit bisette [used].- Chaucer.

Of smale houndes hadde she, that sche fedde With rosted flessh, or mylk and wastel breed.-Id.

This ending has now dropped off, leaving some weak verbs with the same form throughout: as set, set, set; put, put, put.

Irregular Weak Verbs- Class I

Present Tense.	Past Tense.	Past Participle.
bereave	bereft, bereave	bereft, bereaved
beseech	besought	besought
burn	burned, burnt	burnt
buy	bought	bought
catch	caught .	caught
creep	crept	crept
deal	dealt	dealt
dream	dreamt, dreamed	dreamt, dreamed
dwell	dwelt	dwelt
feel	felt	felt
flee	fled	fled
have	had	had (once haved)

hide	hid	hidden, hid
keep	kept	kept
kneel	knelt	knelt
lay	laid	laid
lean	leaned, leant	leaned, leant
leap	leaped, leapt	leaped, leapt
leave	left	left
lose	lost	lost
make	made (once maked)	made
mean	meant	meant
pay	paid	paid
pen [inclose]	penned, pen	penned, pent
say	said	said
seek	sought	sought
sell	sold	sold
shoe	shod	shod
sleep	slept	slept
spell	spelled, spelt	spelt
spill	spilt	spilt
stay	staid, stayed	staid, stayed
sweep	swept	swept
teach	taught	taught
tell	told	Told

think	thought	Thought
weep	wept	Wept
work	worked, wrought	worked, wrought

Irregular Weak Verbs- Class I

Present Tense.	Past Tense.	Past Participle.
bend	bent, bended	bent, bended
bleed	bled	Bled
breed	bred	Bred
build	built	Built
cast	cast	Cast
cost	cost	Cost
feed	fed	fed
gild	gilded, gilt	gilded, gilt
gird	girt, girded	girt, girded
hit	hit	hit
hurt	hurt	hurt
knit	knit, knitted	knit, knitted
lead	lad	led
let	let	let
light	lighted, lit	lighted, lit
meet	met	met
put	put	put
quit	quit, quitted	quit, quitted

read	read	read
rend	rent	rent
rid	rid	rid
send	sent	sent
set	set	set
shed	shed	shed
shred	shred	shred
shut	shut	shut
slit	slit	slit
speed	sped	sped
spend	spent	spent
spit	spit [obs. spat]	spit [obs. spat]
split	split	split
spread	spread	spread
sweat	sweat	sweat
thrust	thrust	thrust
wed	wed, wedded	wed, wedded
wet	wet, wetted	wet, wetted

There seems to be in Modern English a growing tendency toward phonetic spelling in the past tense and past participle of weak verbs. For example, -ed, after the verb bless, has the sound of t: hence the word is often written blest. So with dipt, whipt, dropt, tost, crost, drest, prest, etc. This is often seen in poetry, and is increasing in prose.

In Anglo-Saxon times there were seven 'classes' of strong verbs, which were distinguished by the series of vowels that were used in the various forms of the verb. The modern English past tense of 'to sing' is 'sang', but the past tense of 'to think' is not 'thank'. This seeming difference occurs because the verbs belong to different classes of strong verbs.

In the past there were far more strong verbs in the language than there are today. Some verbs have gradually just been turned into weak verbs by the abandonment of the old system of root vowel modification and the substitution of the -ed ending. New verbs that have been coined or been borrowed from other languages have usually simply been given the weak form. An example of a strong verb that has been converted into a weak verb is 'to glide', whose past form used to be 'glad'. Rarely, a borrowed verb comes to have a strong form. One such example is the verb 'to catch' which was borrowed from French, and today has what appears to be a strong form.

Interestingly, there are a few verbs that have fluctuated between forms, for example 'to dive'. In the Anglo-Saxon period, this verb had both weak and strong forms. In much of the Modern English period, it was a weak verb. In some areas it has recently re-acquired the past tense form 'dove'. The form dove was considered only a dialectic, non-standard form just a century ago; today childrenare in many regions regularly 'corrected' if they say 'dived'.

Throughout history English speakers have gradually been dropping the use of the strong form of verbs. Estimates vary, but there is general agreement that in the Old English period there were over 300 strong verbs. Today, there are less than one hundred, including borrowed words that have taken on strong forms. Although there are occasional complications, as in the case of to dive, it is likely that the language will continue to move toward the weak form. Someday we may all say 'I thinked about it but she had already singed it, so I taked the day off and went to the lake and swimmed.'

13

Mood in Verbs

Mood in verbs refers to one of three attitudes that a writer or speaker has to what is being written or spoken. The indicative mood, which describes most sentences on this page, is used to make a statement or ask a question. The imperative mood is used when we're feeling sort of bossish and want to give a directive, strong suggestion, or order:

— Get your homework done before you watch television tonight.

— Please include cash payment with your order form.

— Get out of town.

Notice that there is no subject in these imperative sentences. The pronoun you (singular or plural, depending on context) is the "understood subject" in imperative sentences. Virtually all imperative sentences, then, have a second person (singular or plural) subject. The sole exception is the first person construction, which includes an objective form as subject: "Let's (or Let us) work on these things together."

The subjunctive mood is used in dependent clauses that do the following:

1) express a wish;
2) begin with if and express a condition that does not exist (is contrary to fact);
3) begin with as if and as though when such clauses describe a speculation or condition contrary to fact; and
4) begin with that and express a demand, requirement, request, or suggestion.

A new section on the uses of the Conditional should help you understand the subjunctive.

— She wishes her boyfriend were here.

— If Juan were more aggressive, he'd be a better hockey player.

— We would have passed if we had studied harder.

— He acted as if he were guilty.

— I requested that he be present at the hearing.

The subjunctive is not as important a mood in English as it is in other languages, like French and Spanish, which happen to be more subtle and discriminating in hypothetical, doubtful, or wishful expressions. Many situations which would require the subjunctive in other languages are satisfied by using one of several auxiliary verbs in English.

The New York Public Library's Writer's Guide to Style and Usage has this important note on the subjunctive: "The words if, as if, or as though do not always signal the subjunctive mood. If the information in such a clause points out a condition that is or was probable or likely, the verb should be in the indicative mood. The indicative tells the reader that the information in the dependent clause could possibly be true".

The present tense of the subjunctive uses only the base form of the verb.

— He demanded that his students use two-inch margins.

— She suggested that we be on time tomorrow.

The past tense of the subjunctive has the same forms as the indicative except (unfortunately) for the verb to be, which uses were regardless of the number of the subject.

— If I were seven feet tall, I'd be a great basketball player.

— He wishes he were a better student.

— If you were rich, we wouldn't be in this mess.

— If they were faster, we could have won that race.

USING VERB MOODS

Verbs may be in one of three moods: indicative, imperative, or subjunctive. The indicative mood is used to make factual statements. The imperative mood makes a request or a command. The subjunctive mood can express a doubt or a wish using clauses beginning with "if" or "that"; it can also express a request, demand, or proposal in a clause beginning with "that."

The Indicative Mood

The indicative mood is the most common and is used

to express facts and opinions or to make inquiries. Most of the statements you make or you read will be in the indicative mood.

The highlighted verbs in the following sentences are all in the indicative mood:

– Joe picks up the boxes.
– The german shepherd fetches the stick.
– Charles closes the window.

The indicative represents something as a fact:

By declaring a thing to be true or not to be true.

Examples

1. Distinction is the consequence, never the object, of a great mind (Allston).
2. The children go to bed early.
3. I do not remember when or by whom I was taught to read.
4. He writes legibly.
5. Taj Mahal is in Agra.

By assuming a thing to be true without declaring it to be so, that is, expressing a supposition which is assumed as a fact.

Examples

1. If you invite me, I shall come.
2. If it snows, I shall make a snowman.
3. If he is the culprit, he should be punished.
4. If you need it urgently, just say so.
5. If wishes were horses, beggars would ride them.

By asking a question to find out facts.

Examples

1. Is private credit the friend the patron of industry?
2. With respect to novels what shall I say?
3. Are you interested in this book?
4. Do you smoke?
5. Is the loft high?

The Imperative Mood

The imperative mood is also common and is used to give orders or to make requests. The imperative is identical in form to the second person indicative.

The highlighted verbs in the following sentences are all in the imperative mood:

— Pick up those boxes.

— Fetch.

— Close the window.

The imperative is naturally used mostly with the second person, since commands are directed to a person addressed.

a) Command

Examples

1. Honour all men; love all man; fear none.
2. Come here.
3. Stand up.

4. Call up the shades of Demosthenes and Cicero to vouch for your words; point to their immortal works.
5. Take this book.

b) Entreaty

Examples

1. Have mercy upon us.
2. Oh, from these sterner aspects of thy face.
3. Spare me and mine, nor let us need the wrath.
4. Of the mad unclaimed elements.
5. Help me with this task.
6. Give us this day our daily bread.
7. Forgive me my sins.

c) Exhortation

Examples

1. Be steady.
2. Take care of your health.
3. Try to do better.
4. Get your homework done before you watch television tonight.
5. Make your request soon.

But the imperative may be used with the plural of the first person. Since the first person plural is not really *I+I*, but *I+ you*, or *I+ they*, etc. we may used the imperative with *we* in a command, request, etc. to *you* implied in it. This is scarcely ever found outside of poetry.

The Subjunctive Mood

The subjunctive mood has almost disappeared from the language and is thus more difficult to use correctly than either the indicative mood or the imperative mood. The subjunctive mood rarely appears in everyday conversation or writing and is used in a set of specific circumstances. The following are the forms of the subjunctive:

Present Subjunctive

a) The verb 'be'

1. I be
2. We be
3. You be
4. He be
5. They be

b) Other verbs

1. I speak
2. We speak
3. You speak
4. They speak

Past Subjunctive

a) The verb 'be'

1. I were
2. We were
3. You were
4. He were
5. They were

b) Other verbs

1. I spoke
2. We spoke
3. You spoke
4. He spoke
5. They spoke

The subjunctive is not as important a mood in English as it is in other languages, like French and Spanish, which happen to be more subtle and discriminating in hypothetical, doubtful or wishful expressions. Many situations which would require the subjunctive in other languages are satisfied by using one of several auxiliary verbs in English. The subjunctive mood scarcely exists in present-day English. You form the present tense subjunctive by dropping the "s" from the end of the third person singular, except for the verb "be".

paints

present subjunctive: "paint"

walks

present subjunctive: "walk"

thinks

present subjunctive: "think"

is

present subjunctive: "be"

Except for the verb "be," the past tense subjunctive is indistinguishable in form from the past tense indicative. The past tense subjunctive of "be" is "were".

painted

past subjunctive: "painted"

walked

past subjunctive: "walked"

thought

past subjunctive: "thought"

was

past subjunctive: "were"

The subjunctive is found in a handful of traditional circumstances. For example, in the sentence "God save the Queen", the verb "save" is in the subjunctive mood. Similarly, in the sentence "Heaven forbid", the verb forbid is in the subjunctive mood.

The subjunctive is usually found in complex sentences. The subjunctive mood is used in dependent clauses to express unreal conditions and in dependent clauses following verbs of wishing or requesting.

The subjunctive mood is used in a dependent clause attached to an independent clause that uses a verb such as "ask," "command," "demand," "insist," "order," "recommend," "require" "suggest," or "wish."

The subjunctive mood is also used in a dependent clause attached to an independent clause that uses an adjective that expresses urgency.

Each of the highlighted verbs in the following sentences is in the subjunctive mood.

— It is urgent that Harraway attend Monday's meeting.
— The Member of Parliament demanded that the Minister explain the effects of the bill on the environment.

- The sergeant ordered that Calvin scrub the walls of the mess hall.
- We suggest that Mr. Beatty move the car out of the no parking zone.
- The committee recommended that the bill be passed immediately.
- If Canada were a tropical country, we would be able to grow pineapples in our backyards.
- If he were more generous, he would not have chased the canvassers away from his door.
- I wish that this book were still in print.
- If the council members were interested in stopping street prostitution, they would urge the police to pursue customers more vigorously than they pursue the prostitutes.

14

'To Be' and Conditional Verbs

Verbs carry the idea of being or action in the sentence.

— I am a student.

— The students passed all their courses.

Verbs are also classified as either finite or non-finite. A finite verb makes an assertion or expresses a state of being and can stand by itself as the main verb of a sentence.

— The truck demolished the restaurant.

— The leaves were yellow and sickly.

Non-finite verbs (think "unfinished") cannot, by themselves, be main verbs:

— The broken window

— The wheezing gentleman

Another, more useful term for non-finite verb is verbal. In this section, we discuss various verbal forms: infinitives, gerunds, and participles.

THE FORMS OF "TO BE"

The Greek sea god, Proteus, was (like the sea)

capable of changing form in an instant. In order to get any decent information out of him, you had to grab him and hold on tight while he went through his various forms – lion, wild boar, snake, tree, running stream – it wasn't easy. The verb "To be" is said to be the most protean of the English language, constantly changing form, sometimes without much of a discernible pattern. Considering that we use it so often, it is really too bad that the verb "To be" has to be the most irregular, slippery verb in the language.

Present Tense

I am	We are
You are	You are
He/She/It is	They are

Past Tense

I was	We were
You were	You were
He/She/It was	They were

Perfect Form	*Progressive Form*
I have been, etc.	I am being, etc.

We must choose carefully among these various forms when selecting the proper verb to go with our subject. Singular subjects require singular verbs; plural subjects require plural verbs. That's usually an easy matter. We wouldn't write "The troops was moving to the border." But some sentences require closer attention. Do we write "The majority of students is (or are) voting against the referendum"? Review carefully the material in our section on Subject-Verb Agreement, and notice how often the choices we make require a familiarity with these forms of the "To be" verb.

We create simple yes/no questions by inverting the order of subject and the "To be" verb.

— Is your brother taller than you?

— Am I bothering you?

— Were they embarrassed by the comedian?

The same inversion takes place when "To be" is combined with verbs in the progressive:

— Am I working with you today?

— Is it snowing in the mountains?

— Were your children driving home this weekend?

LINKING AND EXISTENTIAL 'TO BE'

The verb "To be" most frequently works in conjunction with another verb: "He is playing the piano," "She will be arriving this afternoon." Occasionally, though, the verb will stand by itself, alone, in a sentence. This is especially true in simple, brief answers to questions.

— "Who's going to the movies with me?" "I am"

— "Who's responsible for this mess in the bathroom?" "She is."

In sentences such as these, the subject usually receives the intonation stress and the voice falls off on the verb.

An auxiliary can be combined with the base form of "To be" to provide simple answers to questions that use forms of "to be."

— "Is Heitor in class this morning?"

— "Well, he might be."
— "Is anyone helping Heitor with his homework?"
— "I'm not sure. Suzanne could be."

The verb "To be" also acts as a linking verb, joining the sentence subject with a subject complement or adjective complement. A linking verb provides no action to a sentence: the subject complement re-identifies the subject; the adjective complement modifies it.

— Professor Moriber is the Director of Online Learning.
— Our trip to Yellowstone was fantastic!

In Passive Constructions

A form of the verb "To be" is combined with a past participle to form the passive. Passive verb constructions are useful when the subject of an action is not as important as what the subject did (the action of the sentence) or when the subject is unknown. For instance, the police might report that "The professor was assaulted in the hallways" because they do not know the perpetrator of this heinous crime. In technical writing, where the process is more important than who is doing the activity, we might report that "Three liters of fluid is filtered through porous glass beads." Regardless of the verb's purpose, only the auxiliary form of "To be" changes; the participle stays the same. The "To be" will change form to indicate whether the subject is singular or plural:

— The foundation is supported by enormous floating caissons that keep it from sinking into the swamp.

— They were constructed by workers half submerged in the murky waters.

Notice how the information about who did the action is frequently found in a prepositional phrase beginning with "by." Passive constructions do not always include this information:

— Wooden caissons were used until fiberglass structures were developed in the 1950s.

— Caissons were also designed to function under water in the construction of bridges.

The "To be" will also change to indicate the time of the action and the aspect of the verb (simple, progressive, perfect).

— Water is pumped out of the caisson to create an underwater work chamber. (simple present)

— Some caissons were moved to other construction sites. (simple past)

— While the water was being pumped out, workers would enter the top of the waterproof chamber. (past progressive)

— Many other uses of caisson construction have been explored. (present perfect)

— Caissons had been used by the ancient Romans. (past perfect)

— Other uses will be found. (future)

The "To be" verb can be combined with other modal forms (along with the past participle of the main verb) to convey other kinds of information.

— The wall joints may be weakened if the caissons can't be rebuilt.

- Perhaps the caissons should be replaced; I think they ought to be.
- These ancient, sturdy structures might have been rotted by constant exposure to water.

When "To be" verbs are combined with modal forms in this manner, the construction is called a phrasal modal. Here are some more examples:

- Rosario was able to finish her degree by taking online courses.
- She wasn't supposed to graduate until next year.
- She will be allowed to participate in commencement, though.
- She is about to apply to several graduate programs.
- She is going to attend the state university next fall.

Sometimes it is difficult to say whether a "To be" verb is linking a subject to a participle or if the verb and participle are part of a passive construction. In "Certain behaviors are allowed," is "are" linking "behaviors" to "allowed" (a participle acting as a predicate adjective) or is "are allowed" a passive verb? In the final analysis, it probably doesn't matter, but the distinction leads to some interesting variations. Consider the difference between

- The jurists were welcomed. and
- The jurists were welcome.

In the first sentence, the participle "welcomed" (in this passive construction) emphasizes the action of welcoming: the smiles, the hearty greetings, the slaps on the back. In the second sentence, the predicate adjective "welcome" describes the feeling that the jurists must have had upon being so welcomed.

PROGRESSIVE VERBS

The progressive tenses, which indicate something being or happening, are formed with the present participle form (ending in -ing) along with various auxiliaries. "She is driving. She was driving. She will be driving. She has been driving. She had been driving. She will have been driving."

Progressive forms include a form of "To be" plus a present participle (an -ing ending). Frodesen and Eyring categorize progressive verbs according to the following functions:

— to describe actions already in progress at the moment "in focus" within the sentence, as in "I was doing my homework when my brother broke into my room, crying." or "I will be graduating from college about the same time that you enter high school."

— to describe actions at the moment of focus in contrast to habitual actions, as in "We usually buy the most inexpensive car we can find, but this time we're buying a luxury sedan."

— to express repeated actions, as in "My grandfather is forever retelling the same story about his adventures in Rangoon."

— to describe temporary situations in contrast to permanent states, as in "Jeffrey goes to the University of Connecticut, but this summer he is taking courses at the community college."

— to express uncompleted actions, as in "Harvey and Mark are working on their deck."

ORDER WITH ADVERBS

Notice that adverbs of frequency normally appear after forms of the verb "To be":

— As a student, he was seldom happy.

— Arturo is always first in line.

— They were never on time.

Notice that the adverb still appears after "To be" verbs but before other main verbs:

— My brother-in-law still works for the bank.

— He is still a teller after twenty years.

An adverb can be interposed between the infinitive "To be" and a participle, as in the following sentences. The fear of splitting an infinitive is without grounds in this construction.

— This medicine has to be carefully administered.

— She turned out to be secretly married to her childhood sweetheart.

UNNECESSARY USES OF "TO BE"

Even a casual review of your writing can reveal uses of the verb "To be" that are unnecessary and that can be removed to good effect. In a way, the "To be" verb doesn't do much for you — it just sits there — and text that is too heavily sprinkled with "To be" verbs can feel sodden, static. This is especially true of "To be" verbs tucked into dependent clauses (particularly dependent clauses using a passive construction) and expletive constructions ("There is," "There were," "it is," etc.). Note that the relative pronoun frequently disappears as well when we revise these sentences.

— He wanted a medication that was prescribed by a physician.

— She recognized the officer who was chasing the crook.

— Anyone who is willing to work hard will succeed in this program.

— It was Alberto who told the principal about the students' prank. (Notice that the "it was" brought special emphasis to "Alberto," an emphasis that is somewhat lost by this change.)

— A customer who is pleased is sure to return. A pleased customer is sure to return. (When we eliminate the "To be" and the relative pronoun, we will also have to reposition the predicate adjective to a pre-noun position.)

An expletive construction, along with its attendant "To be" verb, can often be eliminated to good effect. Simply omit the construction, find the real subject of the sentence, and allow it to do some real work with a real verb.

— There were some excellent results to this experiment in social work. (Change to . . . .) This experiment in social work resulted in . . .

— There is one explanation for this story's ending in Faulkner's diary. (Change to . . . .) Faulkner's diary gives us one explanation for this story's ending.

On the other hand, expletive constructions do give us an interesting means of setting out or organizing the work of a subsequent paragraph:

– There were four underlying causes of World War I. First, ...

TAG QUESTIONS WITH "TO BE"

When we use "To be" verbs in a tag question, the basic formula follows: the verb is combined with a pronoun and sometimes with *not* (usually in a contracted form). Positive statements are followed by negative tags; negative statements by positive tags.

– Robert Frost was America's favorite poet, wasn't he?

– He wasn't widely accepted in this country at first, was he?

– You were going to skip this poem, weren't you?

– There were several typographical errors in this anthology, weren't there? (Be careful here. It's not "weren't they.")

– I am not a very good reader, am I?

– I'm a better reader than you, aren't I?

Don't try to make sense of this last construction. It is acceptable. In *very* formal text, you might write "am I not" instead. "Ain't" is not regarded as acceptable except in text attempting to duplicate substandard speech.

FUZZY VERB PHRASES WITH "BE"

Verb phrases containing "be" verbs are often merely roundabout ways of saying something better said with a simple verb. Thus "be supportive of" for "support" is verbose.

The following circumlocutory uses of "be" verbs are common in stuffy writing. The simple verb (in parentheses) is usually better:

— be abusive of (abuse)
— be applicable to (apply to)
— be benefited by (benefit from)
— be derived from (derive from)
— be desirous of (desire or want)
— be determinative of (determine)
— be in agreement (agree)
— be in attendance (attend)
— be indicative of (indicate)
— be in error (err)
— be in existence (exist)
— be influential on (influence)
— be in possession of (possess)
— be in receipt of (have received)
— be in violation of (violate)
— be operative (operate)
— be productive of (produce)
— be promotive of (promote)
— be supportive of (support)

Many such wordy constructions are more naturally phrased in the present-tense singular: "is able to" ("can"), "is authorized to" ("may"), "is binding upon" ("binds"), "is empowered to" ("may"), "is unable to" ("cannot").

STATIVE AND DYNAMIC FORMS

Martha Kolln suggests that we think of the difference between stative and dynamic in terms of "willed" and "nonwilled" qualities. Consider the difference between a so-called dynamic adjective (or subject complement) and a stative adjective (or subject complement): "I am silly" OR "I am being silly" versus "I am tall." I have chosen to be silly; I have no choice about being tall. Thus "Tall" is said to be a stative (or an "inert") quality, and we cannot say "I am being tall"; "silly," on the other hand, is dynamic so we can use progressive verb forms in conjunction with that quality.

Two plus two equals four. Equals is inert, stative, and cannot take the progressive; there is no choice, no volition in the matter. (We would not say, "Two plus two is equaling four.") In the same way, nouns and pronouns can be said to exhibit willed and unwilled characteristics. Thus, "She is being a good worker" (because she chooses to be so), but we would say "She is (not is being) an Olympic athlete" (because once she becomes an athlete she no longer "wills it").

CONDITIONAL VERBS

The grammar of the lyrics uses what is called the conditional. The writer expresses an action or an idea (hammering out danger and warning and love) that is dependent on a condition, on something that is only imagined (having a hammer or a bell – or, in the next stanza, a song). In this situation, the lyricist imagines what he would do if he "had a hammer" — now, in the present. He might also have imagined what he would have done if he "had had a hammer," in the past, prior to something else happening:

— "If I had had a hammer, I would have hammered a warning."

The conditional is possible also in the future tense:

— "If I have a hammer tomorrow, I might hammer out warning.

OR

— . . . I will hammer out warning."

OR

— "If I were to have a hammer tomorrow, I would hammer out warning."

And, finally, he could imagine what is called the habitual present conditional:

— "If/when I have a hammer, I hammer out warning." [I do it all the time, whenever I have a hammer.]

FACTUAL VS. UNREAL OR HYPOTHETICAL

In expressing a conditional situation, we must be able to distinguish between what is a factual statement and what is a hypothetical statement. (Other terms for hypothetical could be unreal, imagined, wished for, only possible, etc.) For instance, if we say

— "The dog is always happy when Dad stays home,"

that's a simple statement of present habitual fact. A general truth is expressed in the same way:

— "If the sun shines all day, it gets hot."

Statements of habitual fact can also be made in the past:

— "If we ate out at all, it was always in a cheap restaurant."

And conditional or hypothetical statements can be made about the future:

— "I will give you a call, if I fly to Phoenix tomorrow.

(In the future, we could combine the base form of the verb ("give," in this case) with other modal verbs: may, might, could.)

HYPOTHETICAL STATEMENTS

When we express the hypothetical in English in the present tense, we end up using the past tense in an interesting way.

- If you liked tennis, we could go play on the new courts.

(Instead of could, we could have used would or might in that sentence.) The speaker of that sentence is not talking about something in the past tense, even though he uses the past tense "liked." The speaker implies, in fact, that you don't like to play tennis (in the present), so there's no point, now, in going to the new tennis courts.

When we use the hypothetical in this conditional mode, we accommodate our need to speculate on how things could have been different, how we wish things were different, how we imagine that things could be different in the future, etc. In order to express the unreal, the hypothetical, the speculative, or imagined (all those being the same in this case), English has adopted an interesting habit of moving time one step backward. Two verbs are involved: one in the clause stating the condition (the "if" clause) and one in the result clause. Watch how the verbs change.

If the hypothetical result is in the future, we put the verb in the condition clause one step back — into the present:

— If the Bulls win the game tomorrow, they will be champs again.

— For present unreal events, we put the verb in the condition clause one step back — into the past:

— If the Bulls won another championship, Roberto would drive into Chicago for the celebration.

— I wish I had tickets.

— If they were available anywhere, I would pay any price for them.

— If he were a good friend, he would buy them for me.

Note that wishing is always an unreal condition. Note, too, that the verb to be uses the form were in an unreal condition. More about this in a moment.

For past unreal events — things that didn't happen, but we can imagine — we put the verb in the condition clause a further step back — into the past perfect:

- If the Pacers had won, Aunt Glad would have been rich.
- If she had bet that much money on the Bulls, she and Uncle Chester could have retired.
- I wish I had lived in Los Angeles when the Lakers had Magic Johnson.
- If I had known you were coming, I would have baked a cake.

In this last sentence, note the conditional clause in the past perfect (had known) and the result clause that uses the conditional modal + have + the past participle of the main verb (would have baked).

Some writers seem to think that the subjunctive mood is disappearing from English, but that's probably not true. We use the subjunctive all the time to accommodate this human urge to express possibility, the hypothetical, the imagined. (You can review the Verbs and Verbals section for further help understanding the Subjunctive Mood.) Frequently, conditional expressions require that we use were where we would otherwise have used another form of to be. The switch to were is not the only manifestation of the subjunctive in expressing the conditional, but it is the most common.

- If my brother were my boss, I wouldn't have a job today.
- If I were to lose my job, I wouldn't be able to pay my bills. [Notice how this is more uncertain, more "iffey," than "If I lose my job, I won't be able to pay my bills."]

— If I were eight feet tall, I'd be one heck of a basketball player. [The subjunctive is sometimes to express purely imaginary situation.]
— If I should grow to be eight feet tall, I'd be a great basketball player. [This statement seems even more imaginary and unlikely.]

Using Would and Could

When expressing the unreal, the result clauses need would, could or will. The condition clauses do not use those verbs; the condition clauses, instead, use verbs moved one step back in time from the result.

Future Conditionals versus Hypothetical Conditionals

When we want to predict something conditional about the future (what we think might happen), we can use the present tense in the if clause and will or be going + the base form of the verb in the result clause.

— If Jeffrey grows any taller, the basketball coach is going to recruit him for the team.
— If he doesn't grow more, the coach will ignore him.

On the other hand, the hypothetical conditional allows us to express quite unlikely situations or situations that are downright impossible.

— If I boxed against Evander Holyfield, he would kill me.
— If my dad had been seven feet tall instead of less than six feet tall, he would have been a great athlete.

Other Forms of Conditional Statements

The conditional can also be signaled by means of a subject-verb inversion. This inversion replaces the word "if"; it is inappropriate to use both the word "if" and the subject-verb inversion in the same sentence.

— Were Judita a better student, she would have a better relationship with her instructors.

— Had Judita studied harder last fall, she would not have to take so many courses this spring.

Bibliography

Beason, Larry. "Ethos and Error: How Business People React to Errors." *College Composition and Communication*, Vol. 53, No. 1; Sept. 2001. 33-64.

Beissel, George. *A Signal System of Learning Modern English Grammar*. 1985. 1673 Calle Hacienda, Green Valley, AZ 85614.

Berk, Lynn M. *English Syntax: From Word to Discourse*. New York: Oxford University Press, 1999.

Brathwaite, Rudolph. *Writing Through Grammar*. McGraw-Hill, 1995.

Burnette, Dawn. *Daily Grammar Practice*. Peachtree City, GA: DGP Publishing, 2003.

Crystal, David. *Cambridge Encyclopedia of Language* and *Cambridge Encyclopedia of the English Language*. Cambridge University Press: 1997.

DeBeaugrande, Robert. "Forward to the Basics: Getting Down to Grammar." *College Composition and Communication*. October 1984. Vol. 35. Pp. 358-367.

Devet, Bonnie. "Welcoming Grammar Back into the Writing Classroom." *Teaching English in the Two-Year College*, 30.1 (2002): 8-17.

Dykstra, Pamela. "The Patterns of Language: Perspective on Teaching Writing." *Teaching English in the Two-Year College*, May 1997, 136-144.

Epes, Mary, and Michael Southwell. *Mastering Written English: The COMP-LAB Exercises*. 6th. ed. Englewood Cliffs: Prentice-Hall, 2001.

Haussamen, Brock. *Revising the Rules: Traditional Grammar and Modern Linguistics*. 2nd ed. Dubuque, Iowa: Kendall/Hunt, 2000.

Hunter, Susan, and Ray Wallace. *The Place of Grammar in Writing Instruction*. Portsmouth, NH: Boynton/Cook, 1995.

Huddleston, Rodney D. (1984). *Introduction to the grammar of English*. Cambridge: Cambridge University Press.

Kanellas, Robert J., James Carifio, and Lorrain Dagostino. *Improving the Expository Writing Skills of Adolescents*. Lanham, MD: University Press of America, 1998.

Kischner, Michael, and Edith Wollin. *Writers' Choices: Grammar to Improve Style*. Harcourt, 2002.

Kolln, Martha, and Robert Funk. *Understanding English Grammar*. 5th ed. Allyn and Bacon, 1997.

Kolln, Martha. *Rhetorical Grammar: Grammatical Choices, Rhetorical Effects*. 3rd ed. Allyn and Bacon, 1998.

Leech, Geoffrey N. *Meaning and the English verb*. London: Longman. 1971.

Lester, Mark. *Grammar in the Classroom.* New York: Macmillan. 1999.

Morenberg, Max. *Doing Grammar*. 2nd ed. New York: Oxford University Press, 1997.

Noden, Harry R. *Image Grammar: Using Grammatical Structures to Teach Writing*. Portsmouth, NH: Boynton/Cook. 1999.

Noguchi, Rei. *Grammar and the Teaching of Writing: Limits and Possibilities*. Urbana, IL: National Council of Teachers of English, 1991.

Palmer, F. R. *The English verb*. London: Longman. 1974.

Quirk, Randolph, Sidney Greenbaum, Geoffrey Leech, and Jan Svartvik. *A Comprehensive Grammar of the English Language*. Longman, 1985.

Shaughnessy, Mina P. *Errors and Expectations: A Guide for the Teacher of Basic Writing*. Oxford University Press; 1977.

Strong, William. *Sentence Combining: A Composing Book*. 3rd ed. New York: McGraw-Hill, 1994.

Thompson, Geoff. *Introducing Functional Grammar*. London: Arnold, 1996.

Van Goor, Wanda. *Grammar - A Good Beginning*. 4th ed. Largo, MD: Prince George's Community College, 1993.

Vavra, Ed. *Teaching Grammar as a Liberating Art*. Williamsport, PA: Rose Parisella Productions, 30 Marvin Circle, 17701. 1995. right. *The Complete Guide to Punctuation: A Quick-Reference Deskbook*. Prentice Hall, 1st ed. 1988; Ron Jon Publishers, 2nd ed. 1996.

Weaver, Constance. *Teaching Grammar in Context*. Portsmouth, NH: Boynton/Cook, 1996.

Williams, Joseph M. *Style: Ten Lessons in Clarity and Grace*. 6th ed. New York: Longman, 2000.

